LIFE CYCLE

OF

THE

CONDITIONED

MIND

LINDSEY MICHELLE

Life Cycle of the Conditioned Mind
Copyright © 2022 by Lindsey Michelle

Tellwell Talent
www.tellwell.ca

ISBN
978-0-22887-798-1 (Hardcover)
978-0-22887-797-4 (Paperback)
978-0-22887-799-8 (eBook)

TABLE OF CONTENTS

SECTION 4
How Mental Conditioning Affects Us and the Unhappiness That Follows 71

SECTION 5
How We Can Break Free from This Mindset and Live the
Life We Were Meant to Have 87

PROLOGUE

From the time we are born, how we see the world depends on our experiences and what the people in our lives tell us. As we navigate our lives, we choose how to act and what to believe. These choices are heavily influenced by the people we surround ourselves with and whose opinions we value. Some of our choices and behaviours lead us to desirable or undesirable outcomes. We make these choices based on our experiences and the information that is given to us as we are learning.

We form opinions based on the information that we are told. We learn to adapt and live based on rules and consequences in society. We sacrifice our happiness for survival and security. We hide what we truly feel and what we truly think in order to fit into society and the norms that surround it. The romantic relationships we choose to experience may directly result from the expectations we have formed throughout our lives. We may put up with undesirable behaviours around us because we feel that we cannot control our own lives and it is easier to just accept it the way it is.

As we get older, our lives sometimes do not feel like our own, and we often think we have no control over changing the trajectory of our lives for the better. This can lead to feelings of hopelessness and depression. But it doesn't have to be like that. What if we could break the chains of societal expectations and beliefs and finally free ourselves to be the person, we were always meant to be rather than just another face going through life like a machine?

Early Childhood and Behavioural and Thought Conditioning

From an early age, we learn how to act, what to say, and how to feel around adults and other members of society. From discipline and positive reinforcement, we learn what behaviours are expected of us and what behaviours will have good versus bad consequences. Using punishments such as isolation, yelling, manipulation, bribery, and spanking taught us as children to conform and comply with whatever authority figure we had in our lives. As parents, we desire our children to behave in ways that society deems respectful and proper. However, we fail to realize that children are not our property and that we are not meant to control them in that sense. The amount of control that children are faced with often prevents them from truly expressing their feelings and can have dangerous consequences. Children then become afraid of expressing their wants and needs to the person taking care of them because they fear disappointment or feel like they cannot achieve what they want. This carries us into adulthood. We learn that showing negative emotions or expressing negative behaviours resulting by negative emotions will often get us punished. To avoid punishment, we often learn to adapt and change our thought patterns to navigate the world.

When school starts, we learn that our worth as valued and important members of society depends on how intelligent we are and how much we listen to authority. We are taught to trust only the information given to us from authority figures such as parents and teachers and that if we question it, we are wrong.

Our level of intelligence determines whether we earn higher levels of education and receive higher job opportunities. Therefore, our worth as human beings depends on how much we follow societal standards of how information is perceived, understood, and obeyed. There is a level of controlled information that we are given, and if this information is ever questioned, we are often mocked or criticized for our beliefs and our opinions.

CHAPTER 1

Birth, Communication, and Discipline

At birth, we learn to navigate the world. Since we cannot communicate verbally, we use our actions to show what we need. We cry to let our parents know whether we need a diaper change, are hungry or too cold or warm, etc., but sometimes we cry because we just want attention or to be held.

As we grow, we learn to show our emotions by throwing things or throwing a temper tantrum. We have not yet learned how to regulate our feelings or why we feel the way we do. Children will often react spontaneously to what they are feeling; they do not yet understand the difference between good and bad feelings.

When children act out, parents feel they must do something about it by showing their children how to act in acceptable ways. So how do we do that?

Why We Choose to Discipline Our Children

We choose to discipline our children. However, the question then becomes how do we discipline our children? Do we yell at them, take their toys away, give them a time-out, or spank them? Most parents will agree with these punishments.

But let's look at the root of children's behaviours and why parents feel the need to punish their kids for these behaviours. Why do we feel the need to control our children every moment of every day? Is it because this is what we were taught was the only acceptable way? Let's think about that.

We can all remember how we were disciplined as children, which often-included yelling, belittling, coercion, bribery, manipulation, and corporal punishment. These words sound terrible when put together in a sentence, but let's look at how these methods are often used to discipline children.

Raising one's voice is often deemed necessary in certain situations, but it is counter-productive as it only causes children's stress levels to rise. It also teaches children that the only way to get what they want is to raise their voices, which results in further disciplinary measures. Bribery often teaches children that by doing something for someone, the expectation is to get something in return, which goes against what we want to be teaching our children. And using manipulation only bends a child's reality, which is also counter-productive in getting children to behave a certain way.

Children don't understand how the world works, so their emotions get the best of them. They may not know that a toy doesn't belong to them or can't have a specific item they desperately want. When this happens, their emotions take over and are often expressed through crying. Crying is such an undesirable emotion for parents that it is often followed by punishment.

Different Types of Punishments

Often, these punishments involve isolation (time-out), which is typically a way for parents to take the child out of a situation to sit by themselves. This sounds innocent, right? Yes, on the surface, but not if you don't know how to process your emotions properly. This teaches children that expressing their feelings or crying will get them in trouble and that they must process their emotions alone.

But why do we feel the need to discipline our children, and why is the behaviour considered bad? We look to others, the "educated," for guidance, and we blindly accept "standards" as fact, throwing away our instincts because we were raised to believe that societal standards are right and should be followed. If we don't adhere to these standards, we are shamed and told we are bad parents.

We may not want to discipline our children when it comes to something they did, whether at a friend's house or school. But when children misbehave or what is perceived as misbehaving according to others, we feel forced to say things to our children that we don't necessarily want to. This may confuse children because they might not have done something wrong, but it was only perceived wrong because society says it is wrong.

When a child does something wrong, we never assess why the child did what they did. However, if we did, we could discover that it was over a simple misunderstanding. Instead, we look at the act, whether big or small, without looking at the bigger picture.

Do we like punishing our children? No, we don't. Let's say we want our children to eat what is on their plate because societal standards say that they need this type of nutrition to grow healthy, and if they don't get this nutrition, it is considered a form of neglect. So, what do we do if children refuse to eat? Do we force them? Do we punish them for not eating what is on their plate? And what is the alternative? No parent wants to feel as though they are neglecting their children. However, just because societal standards exist, why do we feel the need to obey them? Most parents feel they need to conform to societal standards because otherwise, they risk judgement from others.

However, this goes much deeper than parenting, as societal standards also dictate the difference between good and bad people, which shapes what we should and shouldn't do. But if we break down each layer of a person's behaviour, we will discover there is no right and wrong or black and white; there is only gray.

The Effects of Discipline on Children

So how do these punishments affect children? Children learn to navigate the world by looking to their parents for guidance. They learn to act and behave according to the people around them and what those individuals do to punish or reward them.

Children who are praised and rewarded heavily for listening and complying may become so obsessed with being the best that they often develop toxic behaviours, such as believing they are better than others.

Different Types of Discipline

Let's look at the different types of discipline, and the way we've been disciplined as children affects us as adults. How we've been disciplined as children affects our behaviour and how we think about certain things, but it goes much deeper. It often goes so deep that we are not aware of it as adults. Often, our unresolved or suppressed emotions will cause outbursts in behaviour, and we are unaware and don't know why or what caused them. Others may think we are overreacting, but there is always a reason we feel certain emotions, often because of unresolved feelings. Therefore, when this happens, we must acknowledge our feelings and try to understand why we reacted or felt this way. We must stop telling ourselves and others that they or we are stupid for feeling a certain way. On the surface, it could seem that the situation is not a big deal; however, it is much more significant.

When children get yelled at for expressing what they want, this may cause an internal change in them that says they can't or shouldn't express what they want because they won't get it anyway, or that they will get in trouble, or that it will cause an undesirable outcome. This type of childhood conditioning sets children up to keep their desires inside and not express their needs or wants for fear of punishment or disappointment. This is where many behaviours are subconsciously formed in childhood and why children do not understand why they do certain things. Often when we ask children why they have behaved a certain way, they cannot provide an answer. How do these subconscious behaviours start?

Parents are often told that if they attend to their children's every need, children will cry on purpose to get attention; therefore, the advice given is to leave children to self-soothe to develop independence. But how does self-soothing affect children? Not attending to children's needs creates a lack of trust in children because they feel rejected. Although self-soothing is important in the early months of children's lives, it is also essential to establish that they matter and are cared for and loved.

When children act out, they act out because they do not know how else to express themselves. However, we do not understand this as a society, so this behaviour is heavily disciplined. What is not talked about is the ramifications of disciplining our children based on a natural response and emotions.

Instead of punishing our children and saying they are bad, we should understand and guide our children through their emotions so that they understand why they feel a certain way.

For this reason, when many of us feel like we are about to cry, we often leave the room or feel the need to hide our tears, anger, and frustration. Thus, this makes it difficult to express ourselves properly as adults.

Isolation or "time-outs" teach children that if they don't want to have a time-out and have people around them, they need to pretend to be different in front of others so that more people will want to be around them.

Spanking

What about spanking? Some people are against it; however, some who grew up with it and practice it on their children today will defend it, stating it is the only way to get children to behave. This is often followed by, "It teaches respect."

Spanking is a very controversial subject. Back when it was accepted, spanking was widely used to keep children in line. Unfortunately, children back then did not and still do not have the same mental capabilities as adults. This means they do not understand what is considered acceptable versus unacceptable behaviour (subjectively, of course).

When spanking was highly acceptable, having an unruly child was highly unacceptable. It was also widely accepted that children should obey their parents at every whim, and if a child did not do or say anything that their parents deemed acceptable, they would be punished for it. Most of the time, spanking was effective because it was abuse.

Understandably, we do not want to hear that spanking is considered abuse because it would mean that many of us were abused by those who loved us. However, some may argue that they deserved it and made them a better person, but this is not true. There was nothing wrong with those who got spanked.

Spanking does not make children better behaved, nor does it make them earn respect; we just believe it because it was told to us to justify the punishment. This level of thinking allowed spanking to be accepted for as long as it was.

Why do we do this? We do this because it's a cycle we were taught as children—a cycle that we believe is okay because it happened to us. That is how these methods became widely accepted.

CHAPTER 2

How Discipline and Control Can Cause Children to Act Out or Supress Their Feelings and the Consequences

Children who are disciplined must adapt and do what they are told to survive. This is where many children are taught that they are only good if someone else tells them how to behave.

So, let's look at seemingly well-adjusted children who were disciplined and learned "respect." The truth is, they didn't learn respect; what they learned was to obey those in authority, and if they didn't obey, they would be punished.

Some may think this is okay, but it's not. This only teaches children to follow blindly and not question any authority figure. Have you ever asked your parents, "Why?" and they said, "Because I said so," or, "Because that's the way it is.?" These are the common responses, and they are often used because parents don't know the answer to the question themselves. As children, we are taught to follow the rules blindly, or there will be consequences, and that we should do it because our parents told us to do it, and our parents' parents told them to do it, etc. This is generational thinking.

Looking at the Methods

But how do these methods work, and why are they still used today? These methods work because children are subconsciously taught to listen and obey with the illusion of choice. Parents give their children two choices when they want their children to do something: children can do it and receive a reward, such as positive affirmations, or they can refuse and receive punishment, such as a spanking. However, this is not a choice; this is a cohesion tactic and continues into our adult life.

Parents treat their children like property rather than human beings. Children are meant to explore the world, and sometimes, the world is overwhelming. Therefore, parents must guide children through their emotions to help them understand and process them so that they can embrace all sides of themselves. However, instead, parents tell their children not to express their feelings, teaching them to pretend to be okay when they're not, leaving them with bottled-up emotions. Have you ever heard a parent say, "Stop crying, or I will give you something to cry about," or, "Why are you crying? It is not a big deal!?"

Children who suppress their feelings are rewarded; thus, they learn always to suppress their feelings to please their parents and not get punished. However, children who cannot suppress their emotions end up believing they are always bad, and therefore, they rebel because no matter what they do, they are always considered "bad." Consequently, children become submissive to their parents to avoid feeling like "bad" children.

Confusing Parenting with Control

Parents must understand that raising children isn't about controlling them. Raising children means helping them understand the world and teaching them to use critical thinking and make choices. Once children understand how their choices affect others, the rules will make sense to them, and they are more likely to follow them. However, the problem with societal rules is that they are unfair, outdated, and no longer make sense, and those who are taught critical thinking will eventually question the rules in place, and the rules thus become difficult to follow.

However, if children question the way things are or question authority, they are often told they are not smart enough to challenge these beliefs because they are so widely believed that they are right unless someone in authority says differently.

Children understand acceptable versus unacceptable behaviour based on the actions of those they are surrounded by. Unfortunately, when children are always taught to follow the rules set out by authority but are then told to do something unethical, the portion of their brain that tells them it's wrong is turned off. This is because they are so used to complying that they will comply with something wrong.

How Medications Are Often Prescribed for Children with Perceived Behavioural Problems

When children struggle, or are unhappy with their circumstances, they act out or misbehave. When this happens, parents often assume their children have mental disorders or illnesses that require prescriptions.

Parents often try to get their children diagnosed, which often comes as a relief when a doctor confirms a diagnosis because it gives parents an excuse for their children's "bad" behaviour. This also works when children do not do well in school. Parents can excuse their children in front of teachers and other parents, stating that their child is not on par with other children because of their disorder or illness.

This can cause even more unhappiness and disconnect in children because they think there is something wrong with them, perpetuating even more issues with self-esteem.

We are so quick to give outside excuses as to why children act the way they do that we don't actually treat their problems, which could be trauma or any number of things.

This also happens with adults. We often think we're crazy or there is something wrong with us if we don't agree with certain societal standards, and we convince ourselves we need medication to curb these thoughts and make us feel more normal.

However, these medications only eliminate our natural ability to feel, suppressing our emotions. Yes, these medications might make us feel better, but in reality, we don't feel better; we just feel numb. However, by numbing our feelings with medication, we not only numb the negative feelings but also the positive ones, such as joy, happiness, excitement, and passion.

On the other hand, the opposite can happen. When others with terrible experiences use their critical thinking skills, they manage to break their negative patterning without medication and are often an advocate against the type of discipline they received as a child.

Consequences of Children Who Have Too Much Control in Their Lives

Hence, children become easily preyed upon and manipulated because of their compliant nature. Children are told to listen to their parents, grandparents, uncles, aunts, etc. Children will often see these adults as authority figures, and without any means of thinking for themselves, they blindly follow whatever they are told based on the fear of consequences.

How often do we hear about childhood sexual abuse? Children are taught to be so compliant that when abuse happens, they suppress their emotions for fear of being punished; thus, the vicious cycle continues.

The Importance of Children Expressing Their Feelings without the Fear of Judgement and Punishment

Society needs to normalize the expression of feelings and remove the shame associated with doing so. Giving children safe spaces to talk and validate their emotions will help stop them from bottling their emotions up inside. We need to normalize that acting out is okay if we can properly express our feelings.

Parents need to watch for signs of stress when children are left alone with adults. If children are stressed about being alone with an adult, it doesn't necessarily mean they are being abused; it just may mean they are uncomfortable or prefer to stay with the parent. This is often the case with babysitters or day homes/daycares. Children are put into new situations where they are unsure how to act, and they don't know the rules. Thus, parents must communicate expectations to their children.

Believing Your Child When They Disclose Their Feelings about a Person or Situation

Often parents will dismiss their children as liars and not take them seriously. This will often encourage children not to come forward. There are many types of abuse, and parents must realize that children are susceptible to facing emotional and mental abuse from other adults and children.

Has your child ever told you that another adult, teacher, or child yelled at them? What was your response? Typically, parents respond by asking their children what it was that they did wrong to warrant them getting yelled at. However, why are we inclined to blame the child that is getting yelled at? By doing so, children are less likely to report abuse because they are taught to believe that they deserved it.

Children who do not have a strong sense of self will often take name-calling to heart. This psychological abuse affects us as adults because we don't develop a sense of self; instead, we base our opinion of ourselves on how others perceive us. This can also be generational thinking because we see our parents acting the same way.

Therefore, it is important for children to express their feelings without the fear of judgement and punishment. By giving children safe spaces to express themselves, we can build a strong next generation.

CHAPTER 3

School and Control in Elementary

When children transition to a school setting, new authority figures are introduced. However, unlike parents, teachers cannot spank children; instead, they control them with grades or withdraw help from them.

Children are then taught that they must believe and reiterate all information that their teachers teach, and if they do not, they get a low grade. However, many assignments are subjective and can be marked wrong if a teacher doesn't like the answer. As a result, children become mindless robots, only absorbing the information that the teacher deems necessary.

Schools often only show one way of thinking, so when children question the information teachers provide, the teachers often respond by saying that it is just the way it is. Teachers have been taught in the same way, so it becomes a vicious cycle.

How Teachers and Early Education/Childhood Can Diminish a Child's Self-Esteem and Self-Worth Regarding Their Intelligence

Even though some children may not get answers completely right but show a different understanding, teachers will disregard their answers. Teachers often look at answers objectively rather than subjectively, which is a major problem in schools. As a result, children get misdiagnosed as cognitively delayed or impaired; they are not given credit for processing problems differently.

Children should be allowed to play, explore, ask questions, and use their imaginations. Instead, they are bombarded with things that they must do with no control over what they would like to do. They spend most of their time in school complying with the rules and then complying with their parents' rules at home. A lot of the time, children don't have a chance to breathe.

Parents will often pressure their children to do well in school because society places high importance on education. However, sometimes children do not do well in school, and their parents put more pressure on them to do better, leading them to give up altogether when they don't get the results.

When children try hard to get good grades but still get criticized for their lack of effort and poor grades, it affects them greatly. They become self-aware that their efforts will often lead to nowhere, and they lose faith in themselves. If children get to this point, it is difficult to get them out of this mindset. Often, parents repeat behaviours they have grown accustomed to; this is generational thinking.

How We Are Taught from a Young Age to Trust the Information from Educators and to Never Question or Challenge It

Teachers are taught that the curriculum they offer students is the correct curriculum. They are instructed to teach students and instil in them some beliefs they might not learn at home. Children are told to trust and believe their teachers because the teachers are considered educated individuals, and when someone is educated, they automatically become a beacon of information that must be trusted and never questioned.

However, this is a dangerous mindset because information and validity of information are fluid and change all the time depending on the different experiences people have. Not one piece of information is one hundred percent true as we are taught. Information can be stated as true and accepted as true if enough people believe it is true. Therefore, when we learn information as children, we begin to believe it is true without exploring whether it is correct.

However, like parents, teachers have their own thoughts about the world, which significantly impacts what children are taught in school. If a teacher believes in a certain philosophy, they may use examples of that philosophy in class and unknowingly push a certain belief onto their students. This often makes it difficult for children to receive an unbiased education. If children challenge their teachers' beliefs, they will receive lower grades due to their teachers' inability to see a different side.

Children are learning machines; they soak up information. Sometimes, the information they are presented in school conflicts with what they are taught at home, leaving them confused. Teachers also struggle with teaching because they fear their reputation or credibility will be questioned if children do not do well in their class. Therefore, they often tell parents it's their children's fault for not absorbing the information. However, sometimes, children are not interested in the subject and don't have the natural ability to excel in certain topics. If this is the case, the best thing to do is find something that the children are interested in and use their interests to help with the learning process.

CHAPTER 4

The Pressure of Future Education and Endeavours in University

After high school, teenagers feel pressured to figure out what they want to do with the rest of their lives. They feel pressured to pick a suitable career and one that will make them money, regardless of whether it's something they want to do.

This is often a difficult time for teenagers because they are transitioning to adults, and when this happens, especially for those heavily influenced by the adults in their lives, making choices for themselves is difficult. This is when many teenagers choose careers that please their parents instead of careers they wish to have.

Many teenagers do not know what they want to do, and they are not given a chance to discover it for themselves because they are told that they need to decide quickly, and this decision is often one they will change later in life. This is especially difficult for those who do not want to go to university but feel they are forced even though they are legally an adult and can legally make their own decisions. Often, parents and family members have a hold on them regarding their future arrangements.

How Future Choices Regarding Further Education Can Affect How a Young Adult Is Seen by Society and the People in Their Life

If their children go to a good school or land a good job, parents see this as a form of accomplishment. The inverse is true if children do not attend a good school or land a good job. In this case, parents often believe they have failed.

If children choose to be doctors, lawyers, or work in the corporate world, they are considered successful. However, if children want to go the artistic route and work for themselves, this is considered risky and not the path to success. On the surface, this may sound scary, but these career choices are often the most rewarding because one can control what they do and how they do it.

However, society is built to have everyone work in the corporate world and be controlled. The establishment does not want free-thinking people that can be independent and work on their own. They need to keep people in the thought pattern that they need money and a good job to survive.

Teenagers often feel forced to go to university rather than take a year off to figure it out. However, when teenagers choose to take a year off, they are often not supported by their parents. How much support parents give their children is another reason many teenagers will choose to go to university even though they don't want to. However, they never get the chance to figure out who they are and what they want. They never get asked whether their decision will make them happy.

How We View Ourselves and Our Abilities Affect What We Choose to Pursue as a Career

Our ambitions are often geared toward what we *believe* we are capable of rather than what we are capable of, and our views are limited to what we think we can make money doing. It's not based on what we enjoy doing or are passionate about. It is about how much money we can make.

We have heard it all before from our parents and society: to be successful, we need a good education to get a good job. Yes, education is important, but no one ever talks about those who didn't attend university and have become successful. From an early age, teachers instill in us that an education and a good job will get us what we need in life. The problem is that many careers are extremely successful that do not require education, but teachers, parents, and society do not encourage this. Instead, we are often discouraged by others to venture off and do something different because of the lack of stability. The fear that we won't be able to support our family keeps us in a safe work option with little to no growth. Therefore, many jobs that pay well are pushed when teenagers graduate school. We are forced to think about stable jobs that pay, and most of these jobs require an excellent education and a university degree. These careers often require high grades and over a decade of education.

Our lives are predetermined by our parents and our teachers in many ways based on how well we listen and retain information. Schools teach us to get used to the idea that there will always be an authority figure in our lives. It is socially acceptable to work for someone else our entire lives. Society will downplay how possible it is to work for oneself, and many will believe that it is just out of their reach and that they could never achieve self-employment. Most schools prepare students to listen to and obey their bosses in the corporate world. In many job settings, employees are treated like children in school. They are told when to eat, go to the bathroom, and when to speak or stay quiet. Someone with less knowledge can yell at adults because they are an authority figure.

How People Are Judged on How Successful They Are Because of Their Education Status

Furthermore, there is judgement around those who do not attend university; others may think they are unintelligent or do not make enough money. This can often cause a divide between people, leaving those without an education feeling bad about themselves. However, this is the problem with today's society. Just because someone can reiterate recycled information being presented generation over generation does not mean they are more educated. Many people in this world can memorize facts from textbooks and understand and reiterate the information given to them. But how many of us read something that everyone else deems true and sit with it and ask ourselves why?

Unfortunately, it is mostly the educated who have trouble seeing new perspectives and being open to new ideas. This is because they are taught that only information from teachers and books is correct, and if that information doesn't fit into that box, it is incorrect and should be discarded.

Sometimes, those who do not get good grades or spend a decade in school often find themselves in low-paying jobs, leaving them feeling disempowered and resenting their work. They begin to feel trapped and unable to make their own choices because they need to make money. Their hands are tied; they must follow orders regardless of their beliefs to pay for their family's needs. This can be exhausting and emotionally demanding, and this is not something anyone should have to endure.

CHAPTER 5

Controlled Information

Controlled information has become a major problem in our society. We are not taught what goes on; rather, we are taught what society wants to teach us. There is a level of controlled information under the guise of relevant information; we are only taught what is relevant to our society.

What does this mean? This means that we are only entrusted with the information that higher education can teach us. This is because any other information that does not constitute as important is not taught. But what is this other information?

How We View Correct versus Incorrect Information

What if the information we are not taught allows us to think differently? Some might argue that it isn't correct information; therefore, it is not taught, but what if it isn't incorrect information? What if it is information that challenges the current information that is taught in educational institutions? What if it is information that will challenge students to rethink the way society is run?

Unfortunately, this information is not taught in schools because it is often called misinformation. But what if this information makes sense? What if it follows a pattern that allows it to be interpreted the same way the already established information is taught? Unfortunately, we are told that society wants to keep the same standards and that this information should not be taken seriously since it is not being taught in schools.

But what if people choose not to ignore this information and choose to investigate it further? These people are often seen as uneducated and not to be taken seriously. Their status in education is seen more as a credential than the information they present.

Schools teach the ideologies common in societal standards. This further instils in children and adults how to properly act in society. Under the guise of being forward-thinking, these ideologies push certain beliefs that make people think that if they don't believe these ideologies, they are not good people. However, this is dangerous because a person can still be a good person and not follow what society tells them to believe in.

Furthermore, these ideologies also cause division among people; those who believe in them think the other side is wrong and vice versa. However, there are layers to every thought pattern, and nothing is black and white. There can be bad and good sides to each ideology, so to blindly follow one ideology because society tells us to is dangerous.

One way to bridge this gap is to ask people why they believe in certain ideologies. Is it because they truly believe in them or because they fear being judged or told they are on the other side if they don't?

This can be applied to many aspects of society. How much of what we believe comes from within us, and how much were we taught in school and from our parents and society? This is an important question to ask.

How Controlled Information Inhibits Critical Thinking

Unfortunately, we are so used to people in authority telling us what and how to think that it becomes difficult to switch viewpoints. However, even though some professionals who steer away from the typical information exist, they are never taken seriously because the establishment likes to maintain the status quo.

Maintaining the status quo prevents new levels of critical thinking from emerging. People like what is familiar to them and will not question anything different. This is where the saying "If it ain't broke, don't fix it" comes from.

Sometimes there is a level of understanding in the world that professors and books cannot explain. Unfortunately, this information lays dormant because, as mentioned in the previous chapter, teachers are not allowed to teach anything new. This is very discouraging because it doesn't offer the opportunity for the growth of information. New information or a difference of thought from the original information is scary because it provides instability. If we start questioning the information we already know or believe to be true, it disrupts our ability to interpret the environment around us.

We often use information as a weapon. We use it in conversations to convince others that our views and opinions are valid. We sometimes even quote people of importance or educated status who agree with our stance to prove our point. What we don't know, however, is that whenever there is one stance on information, there is an equally educated person on the other. Unfortunately, we never hear the other side because it is not widely accepted by society, and even though both sides are equally justified, we are often told there is only one side. This can often be found online; with any argument, there is a counter-argument.

Why People Use Misinformation to Discredit Other People's Beliefs and Opinions

However, no matter what side we are on, we will always accuse the other side of misinformation when the information is presented. The problem is that whatever we accuse the other side, they have an equally argumentative way of believing the same for their side.

However, the problem with this is that whatever side is deemed societally accepted, there will be more readily found information because the information is often controlled. The information that challenges what society has in place will always be harder to find. However, this is not because the information that is harder to find is not accurate; it just means that there are fewer people in society that will challenge the status quo.

Often the people who challenge the status quo are those who do not have a higher status of education. This is because they did not follow the only way taught to them in their field.

We see this all the time when people use the argument that this is the way it is. And they get away with it because if enough people believe the information, regardless of the lack of evidence, it automatically becomes truth and is widely accepted as that. This is where we lose our critical thought process. People then have a herd mentality, meaning that if others believe it, they must believe it too.

We live in a society where information is often one-sided, and if we do not sit on the side that society says we should sit on, we are deemed uneducated. People get so invested in their side that they won't even entertain the other.

People will often yell and get aggressive when their beliefs are being questioned, but why is that? Why do people feel the need to be nasty and bully and make fun of someone's beliefs? Why can't we believe what we want to and leave each other alone?

How Television, Movies, and Influential People Shape Our Behaviour and Thoughts

How does what we observe in our lives as children shape what we view as our reality? When we are children, we look to the people directly in our lives—our family, teachers, and friends. When faced with challenges growing up, such as finding friends, we learn to adapt to what others want us to be. Sometimes this will cause a dichotomy in who we are versus who we pretend to be to get people to like us or feel accepted by certain social groups. This can cause us to become two different people or several different people, depending on who we are with and how we present ourselves. This may cause a rift in the parent/child dynamic if control is involved.

How often do we compare ourselves to the people we see in social media and movies? How often do we wish we were that thin and pretty or handsome or rich? How much self-worth have we set on ourselves based on someone we have never met on a screen? Have you ever thought about the strong influence people on social media and celebrities have on children? When teens and young adults try to figure out who they are, they will often be strongly influenced by those they look up to online. But how much of this is real or pretend?

Have we ever changed our personality to what we thought was more desirable to attract the type of friend or relationship we want? Why are we pretending to be someone we are not? Why do we allow other people's opinions to dictate who we like and dislike? How much weight do we put on public opinion when we decide who we should support or not support rather than trusting our instincts?

CHAPTER 6

How Do School and Home Affect a Child's Personality?

A child's personality forms through experiences they have and what they learn, and what is the reaction and consequences of that learning. Therefore, many children are told that they act like their parents/friends.

Children adapt to the surroundings that yield the least negative consequences based on what they value the most. If children value impressing their parents and teachers, they will adapt and will want to impress them by listening, behaving, and thinking in a way that would get them praise. If children do not value impressing their parents or teachers because they do not receive the support or praise they need, they might turn to their peers. However, children might look for validation through all three avenues and balance different views and personalities to accommodate all three. This can become confusing as juggling three personalities to accommodate everyone can be difficult. However, this happens all the time.

How Children and Adults Adapt to Certain Behaviours to Be Accepted

The need to fit in and feel accepted stems from our childhood and mostly from our time in school.

The need for acceptance shapes our behaviour. School can put us in different groups based on how we act, what we believe, what we look like, and what we are good at. This is why school inclusion and a good sense of self are important.

Lower self-esteem in children will often cause them to want to be alone because they fear being judged or not being good enough to hang out with those who seem too good for them. As a result, miscommunication will happen where the other children will assume they aren't liked and retaliate with bullying and segregation.

Creating friend groups also promotes segregation, such as limiting children to birthday party invites or children saying they don't want to play with other children because of differences. When children feel they will be rejected, their defence mechanism is to reject or bully someone first.

Puberty and Challenges with Growing Up

When children reach junior high, this becomes worse. With puberty, children become aware of the different social classes and clicks in school, and they feel extra pressure as their appearance begins to change when puberty hits and their hormones start kicking in. This can be tough on children depending on how well prepared they are for it. However, even the most prepared children could go through a sense of identity crisis, mourning the phase in their lives where they didn't have to worry about this stuff.

Children now have a whole new set of challenges, and they look for guidance in social media, movies, and television, comparing themselves to unrealistic ideals.

Different hormones in kids at this age cause more insecurities that will often also segregate kids based on their looks. Children also start developing the sense of not being attractive to prospective partners or friends they were friends with before. Children may gain or lose weight, explore different hairstyles, or develop acne. Without a good sense of self, teenagers become extremely vulnerable to peer pressure because they long to fit in. This is where "popular" groups are formed.

Teenagers may change the way they present themselves by changing their attitude toward what they think will attract friends and possible partners. They will look to television and movies to tell them how to dress and what to like because that is what is popular. They become a shell to the world to be moulded into whatever society deems important and desirable.

Children often look to others to figure out what is socially acceptable. We are often unknowingly taught how to discriminate against certain people who do not have the same views because we are taught that anyone who doesn't have the same views as us is a threat and a bad person. The problem is that often our experiences determine how we look at things.

Everyone has their own experiences in life, and just because we have not experienced something does not mean it doesn't exist. This is how many arguments start because when we are young, we often have limited experiences other than what our parents tell us and what we see on television and in the movies. A lot of what we see becomes our reality.

As mentioned before, this cycle starts when we are children and ends with us breaking free from what we were taught. This often happens in adulthood because we sometimes see this when we start having romantic relationships.

Trying to Fit in by Being Something We Are Not

Sometimes you will become a person you don't want to be to continue fitting in and being liked. This may include acting a certain way with other social classes, making fun of or agreeing with stuff and people that you don't agree with. This may make you feel uncomfortable, so you may start to believe it yourself, transforming into someone you do not recognize. These behaviours grow because of the widely accepting nature of the group. You may like a movie, but someone from your group may have hated it, so everyone else said they hated it, and you say the same even though you enjoyed it. You may be aware of your lie to them, or you may also change your opinion on the initial review of the movie and convince yourself that it was bad and you were wrong to think it was good.

This is the power of group mentality, and it is dangerous in a teenager setting because many teenagers are so fixated on fitting in that they will often go to great lengths to hide their true selves and become what is accepted to make school and their social life easier. This is often hard to maintain because often, even one slip-up can cause a rift in the social dynamic and all it takes is one person with authority to speak poorly of a member of a group to make that member feel alone and ostracized without knowing why.

CHAPTER 7

How Childhood Conditioning Affects Our Teenage Brain When Dealing with Peers

This is the perfect example of how children would avoid being punished by their parents. They would suppress their feelings to make someone else happy and avoid saying what they want to say because they do not want to face the consequences.

This is how we grow up to have no control over our lives because we are constantly looking for someone else's approval to believe what we think and have our decisions validated. We convince ourselves that we shouldn't feel how we feel, that it doesn't make sense, or that we are crazy to think like that because the only acceptable way to think is the same as everyone else.

However, when you constantly think differently than others and keep it to yourself, you never truly feel like yourself, and this will often lead to feeling that you are not good enough. It is important to be yourself, but many people feel they will lose everything if they tell everyone how they truly feel, and they do not want to rock that boat. Instead, they will continue to be the person that people expect and the person who got them the friend group initially.

Struggling in Your Teen Years to Be Yourself

This can often cause depression and a feeling of unworthiness in teenagers. This person may choose to change themselves and concede to every demand to get back into the group or rebel and not want to be in any group. When someone is exiled from a group, rumours will often start about the exiled person, and that person may lose a reputation or gain one based on what others say, deepening their depression. Or worse, they may start believing the rumours and wondering why they did what they did and regret it. Does it seem worth it now?

Often if a person steers away from who they portray themselves to be, they risk having stuff said about them. This may cause a revelation of what you did to others, and if it was warranted, you might feel bad now. What if those rumours were not true?

This is where we will often look back at our past actions with regret. We have a new outlook on the people we have treated badly and sometimes make amends. This is often seen in movies and seen in movies because it happens all the time.

How often do we spread false rumours or believe something about someone just because one of our close friends or family does? This is what often tears families and friends apart.

Different Social Classes in School

When we approach high school, we have already established which class we are in and associate with the people in our social class. While in these social classes, you are often discouraged from associating with any other social classes, and if you do, you risk not being part of your social group. This is often how racial and social segregation starts in adulthood.

There are people in these groups who believe they are higher than everyone else because that is what everyone in authority tells them, and there are those who believe they will never be a part of this group, so they find people they relate to instead. Some people will pretend to be someone else just to fit in, and these are the people who grow up and are afraid to rock the boat when it comes to certain beliefs, so they just say what the majority says to avoid confrontation.

Often teenagers will feel the need to have parties or drink because of peer pressure. Partying is often linked to social acceptance, as is drinking, because it is seen as highly favourable in television, movies and the media.

Although parents may not like the idea of partying or drinking, they may overlook it because of the popularity status their children have or their child's ability to hide certain behaviours because they are afraid of punishment.

Struggling to Figure Out How to Make Decisions and Control Your Own Life While Still Under the Control of Your Parents

Often children feel the pressure between pleasing their parents and doing something to fit in.

Children may want to rebel when they have overprotective parents. They may feel a sense of freedom in a way they didn't when they were a child, and this may become a form of escapism from their very sheltered life. This could also start as addictions to food, drugs or sex. What parents forget is that controlling their children will have very negative consequences.

Children often do not want to believe in certain things but go along with it because that is how they survive and have their basic needs met. This gives parents a false sense of security because they believe they have raised children with their beliefs, just how they were taught growing up, and how society says parents should raise their children to be proper members of society.

However, children may think differently but hide their feelings from their parents because they are too scared to be judged or punished. This can often cause resentment regarding the relationship between the parents and child and lead to the child rebelling.

When this happens, parents will often say things like, "I didn't raise you like that." Let's take a good look at those words; this is the ultimate power move when it comes to parents. By saying this, the parents' role goes from guiding their child to be the best person they can be on an individual level to instead moulding their child into the person they wanted them and expected them to be.

This is exactly the problem parents have today. They do not know how to separate what they want their child to be from who they want to be. Often parents also look at their children as extensions of themselves to impress others.

Juggling Our Self Image Between What Our Parents versus Our Friends Expect from Us

We live in a society where we are no longer judged on how we present ourselves in society but also on how our children behave in society. Therefore, parents will often get discouraged when their children do not act in a presentable way to the public.

When parents say things like, "You're going to make me look bad in front of others," and tell their children they must do things because their behaviour represents the whole family puts pressure on children.

The child is now worried about presenting themselves accordingly and about presenting themselves in a way that makes their family proud. Why can't we just normalize being responsible for our own behaviour?

As a form of punishing their parents, children may sometimes engage in behaviours that their parents would not approve of because it gives them some control over their lives. Some will do it in secret, and some will rebel in front of their parents to punish them.

When a child cannot express their true feelings, it can have devastating consequences. Other times, the teenager is so oppressed that they never engage in any behaviour that may jeopardize the way their parents think of them. These are often the teenagers who suppress so much emotion that one day something happens where they act out in a way that is so out of character for them that it comes as a shock and devastates everyone.

CHAPTER 8

Why Social Media Influencers and Celebrities Have So Much Pull in How Young Adults Adore Them

We want to have something in common with the people we choose to be around, so we question what we like and dislike to accommodate the people we choose to associate with.

Children who are still trying to figure stuff out will often see what they want in a friend and change to be like them so that they will befriend them. Often these children don't know what they like or dislike or how they feel about a situation or a person; they will often go along with what is popular or what their friends or family or teachers tell them to go along with.

Furthermore, we also learn from television, movies, and social media. Commercials and ad endorsements brought on by certain influencers and celebrities will often promote specific standards, which is why self-esteem issues have become so prevalent.

The influence that celebrities and influencers have is astonishing, but we need to look at the power we give them.

Why We Give Celebrities the Power and Influence Over Us and the Illusion of Celebrities Being Better than Us

We see celebrities as rich people in power as though they are somehow better than us. We see people in power as something that we strive to be. We want to be noticed, we want to have people idolize us, and we want to have the freedom to buy and do whatever we want. Sadly, this is only a fantasy for most, so we live vicariously through them instead.

When someone acquires a specific item, it gives them a sense of entitlement over others. But in the end, it is just a bag or a piece of clothing. The truth is, the lives of celebrities are not as glamorous as they seem. Many celebrities seek alternative means of meaning, which is why many have outbursts and form addictions. They are constantly being controlled by their parents (in the case of child stars) and their managers, and they are not allowed to be completely themselves because they must portray a side of themselves that society deems as acceptable. Otherwise, they will be judged by their audience. This is an extremely large amount of pressure to be under, which is why many celebrities feel alone.

Sometimes the public scrutinizes a celebrity's actions, but we should take a better look at this because we do what we accuse celebrities of in our day-to-day lives. We need to stop putting celebrities down for being human and look at ourselves and our actions and those around us instead.

How celebrities and influencers convince children and adults to think or behave in certain ways

If a celebrity has a specific pull in an industry, their thoughts and ideas are highly recognized as truth. If the public loves a celebrity, they are highly sought after by companies who want them to promote their product. This is because that company knows that if that celebrity promotes that product, their sales will increase. But how much of that has to do with the person promoting it, and how much of it has to do with the product?

Most will agree that they bought something because of the person representing it. It could even be a not-so-great product, but we choose to buy it anyway because of the person behind it. This is also about status to afford the product as well. If you show off a no-name product, no one will care, but it is much more impressive if you show off a product that everyone has seen, but only a few have.

A name is important because it will often classify different individuals as different members of society. We all know that being a wealthy member of society is important to most. Why is this important? Because we are told by those we trust and admire that it is important—that if we are rich, we will be just as important and influential as these celebrities. People buy expensive brand name items because it makes them feel closer to a level of status they wish to have, and certain brand names are associated with the rich.

Why Does Social Media Dictate Who We Can and Can't Like?

When celebrities or influencers get cancelled by the public for doing something that goes against the status quo, we feel forced to unfollow or cancel them too.

But why can't we still follow or admire those who are not accepted by the standards of society? Why do we let others dictate who we can and can't look up to? When we side with someone who has been publicly cancelled, it puts us in a terrible situation because we get judged for it.

How much of the stuff on the internet has been proven to be a lie or a misunderstanding? Lots of stuff. However, instead of looking at it with an open mind and looking at the circumstances surrounding it, we jump to the conclusion that things are true when most of the time, they are not.

How Social Media Can Cause Insecurities and Inhibit Our Ability to Put Ourselves Out There for Fear of Rejection and Public Humiliation

The internet can be a toxic place of misunderstandings and cruelty. Someone may be completely upfront and honest with their opinion on something, and just because it doesn't match our opinion, we feel the need to tear them apart. It takes courage nowadays to put oneself out there.

This contributes to many people not wanting to be who they truly are and not knowing who they are because they are constantly being told how to act, how to think, which celebrity to like, and what influencer to follow. We are being judged now on who we follow, and if the people who speak the loudest do not like who we follow, we are automatically put in the same category as those they don't like.

This is why many influencers are not themselves. Their success is based on pleasing their fan base, and often what pleases their fan base is going along with the mainstream narrative.

Let's look at how what we read and see influences how we perceive certain people and ideas. If we watch the same thing repeatedly from a trusted person on television or a person we trust and adore, and they tell us to follow or trust someone else, we believe them, and anyone who tries to tell us otherwise is lying. This is the hold people have on us when information is so readily available.

This is because people of influence understand their power of influence, and they don't want to lose it. Those who have influence like to control others' standpoints, what is bought in the industry, and who the public sees in a positive versus an unpopular way.

Most of what we see online and in the media is carefully placed there to control markets and information. This is because, with people, there is power. Imagine that if we are willing to unfollow someone because someone we admire tells us to, then what happens when this kind of power influences major world topics?

We often follow the thought pattern of what is popular without a second thought. We often take people's word for it and do not ask for proof.

Sometimes we get so far into it that even when someone gives us proof to the contrary, we will call it fake or question the source. However, it is important to note that often the correct news is the news and information that is not easily controlled by the public.

If news and information are being fed to us from popular outlets, then those outlets are feeding us information to make us behave in a certain way.

The problem is that anyone can write anything they want on the internet, whether it be correct or incorrect. However, it is how these stories get told and the amount of traction they get that needs to be considered.

CHAPTER 9

How Social Media Controls What We Think and How We Feel About Everything

We see this all the time. We are told what bad behaviour is and what is good behaviour. We are told that we are terrible bad people if we are not outraged over a particular trait, and we are asked why when we say we don't like something or someone that is typically portrayed as good.

This happens in movies all the time. There are popular movies and what people will call cult favourites that remain people's favourites forever. Now did we see these movies because while hearing about the plot of a movie we thought wow this seems like something that I will love to watch? Or do we hear media platforms tell us that this movie is phenomenal and that we will love it and that it is the greatest movie of all time.

How Online Media Influences Who We Like and Dislike

Movies and television can push a narrative that the audience can relate to, which is how the audience can be easily influenced to think a certain way. This is how individuals subconsciously could start to not like a character or actor with enough influence.

Have you ever disliked an actor or someone in the public eye that when you were asked why you didn't like them, you couldn't come up with a reason other than being told that you don't like them? This happens to many people in the public eye.

When it is popular to hate someone, and the media wants you to hate someone, that person may be presented with all the characteristics you are supposed to hate. Many people will take that narrative, and because it is such a widespread and popular opinion to hate or despise this person, you will find the majority hating this person.

Or you might pretend to hate this person because if you like this person, you are automatically associated with what this person represents in the media, even though what is being presented is false.

Pressure to Like Something or Pretend to Like It Because of Those in Your Life

Friendships can be lost over this as well, but you must ask whether what you believe is what you believe or what others around you tell you to believe.

Individuals can also go with what their friends and family think just to bond with them, even though their reasoning is based solely on the opinion of someone they love. Individuals may be aware they do not feel the same way but feel they must go along with the person so they don't start a fight or end the relationship.

How Society and Social Media Can Affect Our Self-Worth and Pressure Us to Think and Behave a Certain Way with Future Partners and Peers

This can be dangerous when peer pressure tells you that you are nothing without a partner. If society tells you that you are somehow undesirable or abnormal because you do not have a partner, you may feel pressured to find a partner just to fit into that narrative. It is one thing to attract friends, but it is another thing to attract a person you are now supposed to be in a relationship with.

How do you act? Many teenagers will not act like themselves; they will act in such a way that they see portrayed in adult behaviour either in real life, on social media or on television and in movies. They don't know that this behaviour is very unrealistic and shouldn't be replicated.

The pressure to get a boyfriend or girlfriend mounts, and often teenagers feel that there is something wrong with them if they feel like boys or girls do not want to date them, or they feel that there is something wrong with them if they don't feel the need to have a boyfriend or girlfriend. The pressure often amounts to feeling like you must act or dress in a way that will attract someone to date.

Pressures to Act in a Certain Way in Relationships Based on What Is Perceived as "Normal"

Teenagers are pressured to have someone like them and get a boyfriend/girlfriend, but they are also pressured to look and act a certain way once they have a relationship. Sexual acts are often uncomfortable for inexperienced teenagers, but they might feel they are not normal if they do not participate and are often judged for being too innocent in a negative sense or too experienced in a negative sense. Teenagers will often say that they regret their first experience and wish they would have waited.

On the other hand, if you rush into sexual relationships, there is always a stigma against that as well. The important thing to remember is to only participate in things you feel comfortable in, and peer pressure shouldn't matter. Unfortunately, we look to our peers for authority as it is often a rite of passage for one to blindly follow their peers.

It is also hyped that boys will like you more if they find you attractive, and if they find you attractive, they will expect it, and if you want to keep them, you would have to engage in that behaviour. If you don't participate in sexual activities, you will often feel pressure to not be liked or wanted or feel accepted in your friend group.

More and more teenagers are exposed to sexual and suggestive nature where they feel pressured or obligated to participate because of what is considered normal behaviour. Even though this is not what the teenager wants, it could go either way. They can go along with it and regret it or feel like they were forced, say no, face humiliation, and possibly be out of the social group they worked so hard to be a part of.

How Social Media Can Influence How Others Perceive You in School

We see many shows and real-life scenarios that depict pretty and popular in the same setting, with the pretty girls being what we strive toward. Social cliques start in school based on how you see yourself, whether you are the cool, confident, pretty person or the person with the low self-esteem.

This is where your confidence will either soar or sink. Often confidence and not your appearance or social status will set you apart, but the unconfident are those who will isolate and develop self-esteem issues regardless of how attractive they are.

Often, when you are in the popular clique, you will pretend to be someone or something that you are not just to fit in. This becomes dangerous because you completely change who you are just to be accepted into a group.

Being smart can also be a judgment placed upon teenagers. Smart people can isolate because they feel misunderstood.

This also goes for relationships as teenagers and adults and can often lead to peer pressure. If a child has low self-esteem, they may think that to be worthy of love, they must change themselves or do things they don't want to do. If a child feels forced into sexual relationships because they feel their only value is found there, then this is what shapes them as an adult. If a child feels that being mean to another child or acting out in front of adults will get them the attention they crave, this is what they will do. Often these behaviours are coping mechanisms for the trauma they've experienced.

CHAPTER 10

Thinking Critically About What You Like versus What You Are Told to Like

If we think differently than the majority, we question why we think differently and tell ourselves that our thoughts are wrong because the majority thinks a different way.

What we don't know is that there are people who also think like us but hide it, and we never know this because we are too afraid to communicate our true feelings. After all, we fear the backlash from people and society.

Does this behaviour affect us? Or are we just told it affects us? How much of what we currently believe do we believe because we are told to believe it and because we are so used to complying? Do we believe it, or are we going along with it because we are afraid of being rejected or shunned?

So many of us will participate in talking down or judging another person's behaviour or ideas when they do not coincide with the majority because it is socially acceptable and offers a bonding experience. Most of the time, we will get so wrapped up in other people's opinions that we will fail to gain a second perspective or the other side and will blindly trust the information of the person we trust.

How Failing to Look at Both Sides Can Have Terrible Consequences

This will often prove to be one-sided, cause division, and often leads to bullying. The level of control we give others regarding a situation we know nothing of can end friendships and careers.

How many of us have read or heard a one-sided story and have an emotional connection to it because the person who told us is a friend, celebrity, or influencer we admire? We often become so emotionally invested that we become the people we hate by spreading hateful speech.

This is how targeted harassment starts. If your child is bullied, you automatically believe your child's version of what happened. As such, you may attack the other child's parents instead of getting the other side of the story, which causes division.

We often forget that when we fight for something we strongly believe in, we can behave and speak in a very hurtful manner. We often justify this by saying that the person on the other end deserves it. This is wrong. No matter what side you are on in a debate, there is never a reason to wish harm on another person and rally people against each other.

Justice versus Psychological Harm and Bullying

Justice can be done without physical and psychological harm to the person you are against. We see this type of bullying justified in things we read or see online. We can become emotionally charged, believing a certain narrative and encouraged by people to participate in unlawful acts that are described as justified because of what is shown online.

The people willingly participating in physically and emotionally hurting another based on something shown in the media are so consumed by what the media says that they do not use critical thinking.

If you are being told to be mad and you listen, think about it. What is making you mad? Are you mad because you are being told to be mad? Why are you being mad? How does this affect you? Or are you being told that this affects you?

How much control over our thoughts, decisions, and emotions do social media and others around us have? Could this be twisted? Is it possible that this is not true? What would happen if we participated in this hate campaign and it turned out untrue?

So many times, we find out that what originally outraged us was never true, and then we feel bad and have to apologize. However, those we have harmed may never trust us again. This can also cause irreversible psychological harm to the person that was relentlessly harassed and bullied online over a lie.

The Hypocrisies of Social Justice Crusaders

People who preach tolerance and anti-bullying become bullies, fighting against something they are, which makes them hypocrites. This is what society teaches us: to get upset when we see injustice in the world. But by getting upset, we create injustice as well.

There are always extreme sides to every argument. What often happens is that those on either side of the extreme are typically the most vocal and are often those who spread wrong information because they fail to see the bigger picture. Ironically, these are the people who preach tolerance but, in the same breath, hate those who do not think like them.

These people are under a false blanket of security, but when faced with a different perspective, they deny it because by admitting it, they would also have to admit they were wrong. This is also why it is hard for people to let go of their beliefs, as it is much easier to save face than admit being wrong.

Racism as It Stands Today in Society

Racism is a touchy subject, but today, racism is so highly demonized that it creates division. We need to consider why this is and what we can do to stop the division.

What we see on television and in movies often shapes how we view other cultures and races, and because we mindlessly believe what we watch, this is how many stereotypes are formed. In the past, television and movies gave us false information about different cultures and races. Back then, it was "normal," but as society evolved, we now understand that those stereotypes are not okay and that we need to educate ourselves on racism. However, we also need to understand how deeply ingrained our views were growing up. It takes time to accept that an ideology we believed our entire lives was wrong and that we were wrong for believing it. But this is where the division happens. If we no longer believe the stereotypes we were brought up with and realize how ignorant and foolish we were to believe such things, and society has also come to its senses, why do we feel the need to demonize our past actions? We are now punishing others for something they said in the past. We scrutinize them and cancel them, even though they may not have ever thought that way to begin with.

On the other hand, there are also those who are convinced that because it was widely accepted when we were kids, it should stay that way and that these stereotypes are not racist. However, this is because they can't stand being called racist. Note that those who are most offended believe the racist remarks.

Many people live off the drama on the internet, looking to demonize others to make themselves seem better than others. The irony in this is that these people often do not have clean pasts; in fact, they often have very messy pasts that would be considered hypocritical if they ever came to light.

How Television, Movies, People in Our Lives, and Childhood Beliefs Affect How We See Marriage and Romantic Relationships

As children, we often do not think about who we will end up with and what our life with that person will look like. When we grow up, the pressure to find a relationship builds. If we have never been in a relationship before, we look to familiar things. We may look to our parents' relationship, television, or movies. However, when it comes to these methods of understanding relationships, we find ourselves stuck often in relationships that don't make us happy. This happens when we change ourselves to what we think will attract a partner or keep a partner. We may pretend to enjoy something we don't or may suppress our true feelings about what we feel to avoid an argument or for the person we want to be with to think we are too different and not want to be with us anymore.

Unhappy relationships often go unnoticed because they have become so normal today. The societal standards placed on marriage and relationships often put a strain on the couple. What is traditionally seen in movies is the standard patriarchy that many women are now standing up against. The past patriarchal beliefs that have been passed on for generations have many women feeling unappreciated and overwhelmed.

However, we are not told that we have the control to change our relationships if we are not happy, that happy relationships are normal, and that it is okay to choose yourself over a relationship. It is important to normalize clear feelings and communication when deciding to end or continue a relationship or marriage. Learning what you want in a relationship and properly communicating that will either help mend a relationship or end one allowing a new relationship to take its place that is more emotionally fulfilling and loving.

48

or continue a relationship or marriage. Learning what you want in a relationship and properly communicating that will either help mend a relationship or end one allowing a new relationship to take its place that is more emotionally fulfilling and loving.

CHAPTER 11

Navigating Romantic Relationships

When young adults are asked where they see themselves in five or ten years, the answers are often similar—most will say married with kids, a nice home, and a good career. This is what we all strive toward. This is what society has told us to strive for. And this is why if some do not want marriage or kids, others are shocked. This is often followed by, "You say that now but you will probably change your mind later." In some instances, this is true, but if someone truly doesn't want those things, they will never change their mind. These people are often seen as lonely or that there is something wrong with them. Why wouldn't they want to spend their lives with someone and have kids?

The Pressure to Find Our Life Partners and Have Children Placed on Us by Society and Our Beliefs

Sometimes high school partners will stick around, but other times they will not, and we feel like we need to start over. This thought of needing to start the next phase in our lives becomes so pressured that many of us jump into the first relationship that presents itself, and things often move very fast. This could result in a quick marriage and babies, moving in together, or buying a house. Sometimes these marriages work out, and sometimes they don't. There is often a pull to stay together in these marriages out of shame or discomfort to being without that person. We often convince ourselves that it would look bad or that our lives would be more difficult if we left.

Religious beliefs may also be the result of rushing to get married without fully getting to know each other since some religions don't believe in couples living together before marriage. Many religions push the narrative that women must take care of their husbands and kids. When children grow up in this lifestyle, it is often hard to get out of because it often means that a failed marriage is a failure of God and that they will not only have to leave their husband but also their family, who do not approve of their new way of thinking and behaving.

Often women feel forced to jump into relationships because they feel they are getting old and that their biological clock is ticking, and if they don't get married and settle down soon, they will miss their chance to have a family and the life they think they want—a life that the media and society tell them they should have.

Misconceptions about the Importance of Marriage and the Consequences that Follow

What if marriage is not the goal, and some just enjoy the relationship? Often a couple will feel pressure to get married because that is what everyone else wants, which results in broken expectations.

Because of the pressure to find a partner in our twenties, we often change our personalities to attract a partner. We look at what society deems worthy or desirable and aspire to be that person. A couple then enters a relationship based on false pretenses.

Women also feel the need to compete with their friends to see who will get married, buy a house, or have babies first. Our worth as women often depends on these factors, and if we see other women with things we don't have, we often feel inadequate and push ourselves to settle for a relationship we don't want and convince ourselves otherwise.

Often, the couple may feel trapped in the relationship, and they are willing to overlook things they shouldn't. Sometimes they even convince themselves that it is their fault and that their standards are too high and that they should be grateful to have a husband or wife and the life they have because this is what others want but don't have.

Marriage sometimes works, but it also sometimes fails. This is often dependent on the emotional maturity of each partner. A marriage that is rich in communication and equal give and take will have a better long-lasting standing than a marriage where each partner does not express their needs and disregards the other's feelings.

A Persons Desire to Change Themselves to Attract a Partner

A woman may change her appearance to attract a partner based on what society has said is desirable. If the woman or man does not feel they can live up to these beauty standards, they may feel unworthy. This is a false reality that many women and even men have.

The truth is that everyone deserves to be loved. No one is perfect, and no one should pretend to be perfect. It is our flaws and our likes and dislikes that make us unique. Our flaws are what we see. Often our flaws bother us more than who we are dating. We should never pretend to like or dislike something just to fit in or be liked because it is not attainable and could result in the other person feeling like we are being fake or unauthentic.

If we are openly honest about our past, our likes and dislikes, and what we want in a relationship, and the other person feels the same or is willing to give the relationship a try, then the relationship is already off to a great start. But this can also go the other way where the other person does not want the same things, and they decide that they do not want to pursue a relationship. This choice also needs to be respected. This can become very problematic when someone in the couple pretends to be someone they are not so that the other will continue to date them or eventually marry them. However, this takes a toll on the person pretending because they are constantly trying to act in ways that please their partner, and eventually, this can lead to an outburst. The best way to avoid this is to always stay true to ourselves and be authentic.

Children and Adults View Relationships Based on What They Experience in Life and What They See on Social Media, Television, and Movies

Our family dynamics affect how we view healthy relationships. If our mothers always did the cooking, cleaning, and child care, and our fathers worked, then we might consider this normal. However, what we don't know is how much our parents held in and didn't express to us.

It is also important to know that what we observe from television and movies can affect what we expect in relationships when this isn't the case.

When we start dating, we have nowhere to go for reference, so how we approach relationships is often unintentionally guided by our peers and the adult relationships around us.

Television and movies show us what is "common" in marriage. Typically, they show dysfunctional marriages as "common" and functional as unattainable, and this is not right.

Many marriages have problems, just like any relationship. However, it is the level of communication and compassion for our partners, and our collective willingness to work together rather than against each other that will strengthen our marriages.

CHAPTER 12

Women's View on Their Worth in a Relationship

Women may compare themselves to other women and relationships. A relationship portrayed on social media may look perfect on the outside, and someone not in that relationship may look at that relationship and envy it.

Women are often better portrayed and are deemed more desirable on social media. The more men women have at their disposal, the more they value themselves as wife material. However, this puts women in vulnerable positions where they might ignore red flags or subject themselves to relationships they don't want.

Typically, there is an expectation and pressure to get pregnant and have kids with marriage. For those who do not want this, it becomes a problem with family members. On the other hand, if they are trying and can't, it becomes too stressful for the couple.

Many couples dive into having children right after marriage, but this shifts the focus away from the couple. When kids become the focus of a marriage, it often strains the relationship.

After kids and marriage, the picture-perfect life we've envisioned isn't so perfect. The way marriage and kids are portrayed on social medial doesn't often coincide with what our lives look like. Thus, we start to feel the pressure to be happy when we are not, and because of the confusion around why we are unhappy, we try to figure out ways to make ourselves happy. To do this, we must first figure out what we like and dislike about our current situation.

How Lack of Trust and Feeling Controlled Can Affect a Relationship

Often in these situations, one spouse may not trust the other spouse with money, and the other spouse will have to ask for money or be fearful to ask for money for anything other than the children and maybe even still fearful when asking for money for the children. This becomes a depressing and traumatic time for this spouse because they often feel like they have no control in their lives and may feel like a child being told what to do by their parents.

They may feel like they do not want to be in this life, but they have no way of escaping it. A spouse is more subjected to this if this is what they grew up with. Often wives in these types of marriages are used to being controlled by their parents in childhood. As children, they often put on a fake smile and said yes to everything their parents told them to do because they were afraid of punishment and were more likely to listen and never question adults and authority figures. But this is what society wants—a compliant child turning into a compliant adult.

The problem is that often these compliant children grow up and don't know how to manage their lives or make decisions, which puts them in a vulnerable situation when it comes to being controlled by another person. Wives will feel the need to be taken care of, and they feel comfortable having their decisions already made for them because this was what they were taught.

Using Clear Communication to Help Heal Your Relationship and Marriage and How Without Communication, Relationships Can Suffer

However, the problem is a lack of communication. The level of clear communication in a marriage is often based on the level of emotional maturity of both people involved. A couple with high emotional maturity will understand and process their own feelings and their partner's feelings. If there is something they feel is unfair, they will communicate it to their partner in a loving way and understand the other's perspective. Thus, they will reach a peaceful resolution.

When both people in the couple have very low emotional maturity, their marriage often becomes toxic because they lack empathy for the other and lack understanding. This may also cause insecurities in the relationship where one believes the other hates them or is not sexually attracted to them when it is something completely different.

The lack of physical intimacy is a big factor in ending a relationship. However, people do not realize that when there is a lack of physical intimacy, it is because there is often a lack of emotional intimacy. Physical intimacy can be fun for those who do not want an emotional connection but want to fill a physical need. Therefore, some men and women prefer casual connections.

Others prefer a more emotional connection with intimacy. This is why many people seek out relationships. Relationships often lead to a more authentic emotional connection because we choose to commit ourselves to another.

When the commitment falls apart, and we feel we are not being heard and are not important in a relationship, we lose the emotional desire we had for our partners. When this happens, we may pull away. If physical intimacy is important to our partner, this may be alarming. However, we can't help our feelings.

Trying to Understand Our Lack of Emotional Intimacy for Our Partner

On the other hand, if we do not want to be physically intimate, we might believe there is something wrong with us or that our partner will not understand, so we continue to engage in sexual activity because we are afraid that our partners might get up upset. This can be emotionally draining, and eventually, we may choose not to engage in any sexual activity.

There are many reasons why someone may do this. Most likely, it is because of how they are treated in the marriage. In the case of a woman in a patriarchal household, she may feel that she is more of a caretaker to her husband than a wife, taking on the motherly role with no appreciation. On the other hand, the husband may feel that he is providing for his wife, but it is never good enough. He may not want to be physically intimate, which could lead to feelings of insecurity and thoughts that the other spouse is cheating.

It is important to understand our feelings and properly communicate them to our partners. If our partners become aggressive or mock our feelings, this can cause a bigger emotional disconnect and can cause even more distress.

How Patriarchy in Relationships Can Affect Marriages

Many marriages fall apart because of the patriarchy portrayed in our society. It is often depicted and projected through generational beliefs that women care for the men and take care of the children and house. This system is so highly recognized that outrages happen when women stand up for themselves.

Women are often expected to give up their careers to become stay-at-home mothers and caretakers to their husbands. Because of the stereotypes and how marriages are depicted in society, boys often grow up in this setting, and it sets a generational stereotype that men work outside the house and women work inside the house. However, the patriarchy puts pressure on couples as they both try to do their best in their respective roles. The man may feel pressure to make enough money to support the family, while the woman may feel underappreciated for all the work she does around the house and with child care. Both might feel resentful toward the other for not getting a break.

Many women today are tired of the patriarchy because they are not only expected to take care of the home and their children and husband, but they are also expected to work full-time jobs. The problem is that the men's roles have not changed as they are still expected to come home after work and not help with the kids or housework. This type of behaviour puts a lot of pressure on women to "do it all." How do women get into these types of marriages? Most of us mirror what we experienced in childhood.

If we experienced a patriarchal household growing up, then we will bring that into our relationships.

However, with more women working, this dynamic is changing, and more women are beginning to express how they feel to their husbands. Unfortunately, often what happens due to the deep patriarchal programming many husbands have been exposed to is that they get offended and choose to call their wives names, such as ungrateful, lazy, and lucky (if they are a stay-at-home parent). This often goes with relationships where individuals think they are not good enough, so they often end up in toxic relationships. Patriarchy in a marriage may cause a rift in the relationship when the breadwinner restricts money and privileges from their partner if their needs are not fulfilled. Unfortunately, this is common in marriages and can lead to withdrawal and, ultimately, divorce.

Why women choose to stay in loveless marriages

A lack of confidence in financial security is why many loveless marriages stay together whether cohered or planned. A married couple may choose to live in a platonic marriage for the sake of financial hardship and their happiness with another person, and their goals take a huge sacrifice in the process.

The person who wants out of the marriage may feel like they are not capable of supporting and sustaining themselves and, using the logical side of their brain, may decide that it would not be smart to leave their husband or wife. Some also do not tell their spouse that they are unhappy, and they live their lives in silent depression and agony, wishing their lives were different and that they had a way out.

Financial Abuse as a Means of Control

Because of the stereotypical patriarchy placed on marriages, women often give up on their careers or choose not to have one to take care of their children and husbands. This often puts them in a difficult situation if their husband becomes abusive physically, mentally or emotionally. The men will often understand that they make all the money in the house and will use that to control certain circumstances.

Sometimes in these situations, wives will wish to leave, but they feel they can't because they do not have the financial backing, so they stay for the kids to be taken care of.

This is a common misconception and a common tactic used by men to keep their wives in the marriage. Some husbands can also tell their wives that they won't be paying for them and will be fighting for full custody of the children to try to manipulate them to stay. These women feel trapped but feel forced to stay. These marriages also go unnoticed, with no support or outside recourses. Some women are so conditioned that they don't realize that this is a form of abuse and will never leave.

Others realize that this is a form of abuse but are scared to come forward or tell others because they fear it will come back to their husbands and make their life more difficult. It is important to be there for these individuals as there is no amount of yelling at them to change their minds.

Can These Relationships Be Mended?

The best relationships are the ones where you grow together. It is possible to find the love of your life at a young age if you are both on the same page and choose to grow together. When one stays in one mindset as the other wants to grow, separation occurs. This gets especially messy when marriage and children are involved.

This is because, usually with marriage and children, the word compromise is thrown around so much that we feel that we need to work it out or just accept our life the way it is, which many people do. Therefore, many people in marriages are unhappy or feel they have little choice in their lives. They feel forced to be in a relationship they are conditioned to think is normal and that if they were to end their marriage, they would not get any better and that they would regret it.

CHAPTER 13

Deciding to Divorce or Stay Married

So, if it's normal to feel pressured to stay in a loveless marriage, what is causing women to file for divorce anyway? Because women today are waking up to how undervalued they are in marriage and are standing up for themselves. However, this goes against societal norms, so this awakening is often pegged in a negative light called feminism, which causes rifts between women and men and those who hold old-school values. Those who believe in the old way of doing things believe divorce is a travesty on the sanctuary of marriage, which can cause family members to try to talk women out of getting divorced. Those who hold this view may believe women who ask for divorce are giving up on their spouses. Often when a marriage ends, there is a backlash on the decision. It is important not to give in to manipulation and peer pressure and stand your ground. If these changes do not help with your marriage, be prepared for a divorce. Some spouses or family and friends will often discourage you or try to manipulate you to stay. Make sure that you stand your ground and that your decision is yours and not someone else's. Often what happens in divorce is we feel anxious and second-guess ourselves and how we will survive. For many people, this is a major change in their lives, which is why many couples stay together. The thought of getting out of their comfort zone and not knowing what will happen scares them. This often happens to wives in marriages. This is also very difficult when children are involved. Manipulation tactics such as saying, "You are nothing without me; how will you get money?" "You will get nothing from me if you leave," and "I will take the kids away from you," are last-ditch attempts to control the situation.

Using Compromise to Decide If the Marriage is Worth Saving

Sometimes compromise works, and it is needed in a relationship as long as the compromising person is willing to compromise and does not feel forced. When compromise doesn't work, the relationship is on the rocks, and one person gives an ultimatum that the other must follow if they want to continue in the relationship. This forces the person to look at their relationship and how important the relationship is to them. They will quickly find that if they are not excited about the relationship moving forward and have resentment for the compromise, they must be honest and refuse to compromise and end the relationship.

The problem is that the other partner may see this as a failure or something they did wrong when, in fact, it was a matter of incompatibility. This is not saying that we should give up on every marriage based on a difference of opinion. This is an incomparability based on traits that affect our daily lives and how we love and treat our spouses. And if that trait is causing discomfort in a marriage and the people in the marriage do not feel the need to change or grow with the other person, then it is better for their mental health to end the relationship.

Not all marriages fail. If there is a healthy level of communication in a marriage where both partners are willing to listen to the other and understand what each other needs it can often strengthen a marriage. This usually happens when two people are more in touch with what they are feeling and can openly and honestly express their feelings to the other, and are open to what their spouse is feeling as well.

There are cases of married people getting back together. This is the case of getting married but growing apart. In that separation, both people grow individually and become compatible again. Some may say this is a waste of time and that they should have never divorced; however, sometimes, it is necessary to have experiences that require you to be by yourself to be the best you.

How Childhood Upbringing with Expression of Feelings Can Positively Affect the Way We Communicate and Express Ourselves in Romantic Relationships

This is possible when children are taught to acknowledge and express their feelings rather than bury them. This allows them to have a level of control instead of having their spouse make the decisions and slowly lose themselves. This allows a better mental state for both spouses, and if they choose to end, these relationships often end on good terms.

What often happens in a marriage is that one spouse will want growth and change. Their values and the way they look at things will start to change, and they will no longer coincide with the views and values of their spouse. For example, when a wife who has always been a stay-at-home mom now has the courage and motivation to pursue a career or hobby that she is passionate about, but her husband is not supportive, this can lead to conflict. If both spouses can't grow together, they might "grow apart."

This is where communication is important. Depending on the level of communication and emotional connection between a couple, necessary changes can lead to growing together or growing apart.

Why Do Spouses Cheat?

In relationships that lack communication, one partner may begin to feel trapped and look outside the relationship to fill the void, which leads to cheating.

Some people's self-esteem is so low that they feel they can't get anything else, and the fear of being alone is too great for them. This kind of thinking leads to finding other relationships while in a relationship. Sometimes the person who cheats will cheat because they are still missing a part of themselves, and they, therefore, seek it in other people. However, they will often not want to leave their partner for this other person but rather fulfil a need their current partner can't fulfil. Others will want a new partner, and when they find them, they will leave their current partner for them.

This is where the partner who gets cheated on will blame themselves, but it is not their fault. A person who cheats will not cheat if they are fulfilled by themselves. Therefore, it is important to be whole; otherwise, you will always seek someone else to fill the void within you. Those who are happy with themselves will communicate and be honest with their partner, which creates a happier and more fulfilled relationship.

Staying in a Marriage for the Sake of the Children Will Often Lead to Undesirable Consequences

What often happens is that one spouse will stay in the marriage for the sake of the children so that they won't grow up in a broken home. Most of us think this is the right course of action because we have been mentally conditioned to believe that children should not be raised in a broken home. However, this is not true.

When we stay in marriages where we are not emotionally invested, it often leads to fights and arguments between spouses, thus giving children the wrong idea about marriage. What we tell our children is that marriage involves arguing, not spending time together, and not showing physical affection to one another. This is a much more harmful environment for children to grow up in as opposed to separate homes that could foster healthier relationships in the future.

Often couples stay together for fear that their children will be taken away and they will hardly get to see them. These societal expectations in a patriarchal society could also work against fathers who do not fit in this role. Fathers are often put into the category of incompetence and unwillingness to take care of and participate in their children's lives, but there are just as many fathers who fall into this category as those who don't. Fathers play a significant role in their children's lives, and the roles are often reversed when they are more active than the mother.

The problem is that by society's standards, men's relationships with their children are not prioritized, and in cases of divorce, they are often awarded less time with their children but are required to pay more in child support. This can cause a lot of distress for fathers who genuinely want to be active in their children's lives.

Choosing to Leave a Marriage

The person who chooses to end the marriage needs to know that there is a reason they want to leave a marriage and should not blame themselves for the loss of a marriage. Often if a spouse is cheated on, they blame themselves for not providing the other spouse with a proper attachment to hold onto them. A wife may blame her body after having kids, and a husband may blame himself for working late and not spending enough time with his wife. Whatever reason there may be, it is important to realize that if you were cheated on, it is not your fault. Not all people are compatible; there is no one trait that would set apart another. In most cases, it is just that one trait is not compatible with the traits of the other person and, therefore, the compromise didn't happen because the relationship and that trait were not big enough for the people in the relationship to want to compromise.

The Backlash of Deciding to Divorce

However, regardless of the backlash some women face, they still have the strength and courage to get out of a marriage, even though it is difficult to make that initial decision and take action, and some don't even know where to start. A part of the initial divorce process is for women to be prepared to drastically change their lives. The best thing to do is visualize all the worst-case scenarios and then come up with solutions to them. For example, if a woman is afraid of the financial aspect of the divorce, she can get a lawyer that will help give a realistic expectation of the process.

So, whether you choose to stay in the marriage is up to you. To figure this out, you may want to think about why you feel the way you do and what you like or dislike about your marriage. What changes would you have to make to stay or leave a marriage? Those who change their mind about the divorce will often place conditions on their partner and look for discrepancies in their marriage to dissolve. This may work or fail, depending on each partner's level of emotional maturity and how important their marriage is to them.

Accepting Your Choice to End Your Marriage

A marriage that is headed for divorce is often seen as a death that we grieve. It can go through phases, and one of the changes is to accept that it is for the best and embracing the change you are now embarking on. Divorce can be a new adventure. It can be scary, but it can also be new and exciting. After a divorce, you may revaluate what you want to do with your life, whether it be a new career or hobby. Sometimes it will feel as though you have a new zest for life. You will begin to think about the endless possibilities that you have yet to experience.

Learning What You Want versus What You Don't Want in a Future Relationship

After having experienced a divorce, many individuals better understand what they want in a relationship because they have learned their lesson and now want something different. These individuals often know and value the time they spend alone and, depending on their emotional dependency and maturity, may not feel the need to be in a relationship and may feel they are comfortable being alone.

These are the independent individuals who want a relationship eventually but will not settle for a relationship that is not emotionally fulfilling. This is what happens when you look inside and know what you truly want. For a person to know what they truly want, they need to become whole with themselves.

CHAPTER 14

Fears About Dating after a Divorce

Others may have difficulty dealing with a divorce and will not deal with it in an emotionally mature way. Sometimes these individuals will jump into several relationships to fill a void and feel less alone. Without the process of growth, these individuals will often repeat the same patterns in their relationships.

Others may swear off marriage and relationships because they convince themselves that they will get hurt again. On the other hand, others may choose not to put themselves out there because they fear rejection.

Feeling Insecure After Getting a Divorce

What is interesting is that people will often think that they are less attractive than they are. Someone may think they are out of someone's league, but the other person may think they are out of their league. This is why there is a societal difference when it comes to how attractive someone may be.

Many will think, "How can I find someone who will accept me for me?" "How will this affect my kids?" "Will my kids adjust to this?"

There is an undeniable fear that we will spend the rest of our lives alone once we divorce. This could also be due to our diminished self-esteem that comes from within or results from others.

Women may feel they have gained weight and believe they are undesirable, or they may have aged and feel they need to compete with those who are younger. This is especially alarming since it is socially acceptable for men to date younger women but not for women to date younger men.

However, men also have fears, including feeling that they are only there to support the relationship financially. Furthermore, men might also have self-esteem issues but don't voice them as often.

Often, we may feel unworthy of having a successful partnership. Even if we are comfortable with the way we look, we may have a hard time trusting the other person's intentions. We may question whether they genuinely like us or whether they are taking advantage of us.

However, what if the way we look affects our ability to put ourselves out there? If we do not feel attractive, then we might have difficulty believing the other person's intentions.

How Self Love Affects Our Romantic Relationships

Sexual attraction is one thing; however, we can be sexually attracted based on a strong emotional attraction. But when we question our ability to attract another based on our physical appearance alone, it becomes difficult. We may worry about our weight, stretch marks, moles, birthmarks, hair loss, etc. We can't change many of these things, so it's important not to get caught up in things we can't change; therefore, self-love is important.

Self-love is important in developing healthy relationships. But this is easier said than done. If we only base our worth on our physical appearance, it won't get us anywhere. Confidence is key to loving oneself. Someone could be the most beautiful or handsome person by society's standards and still not believe it when they are told they are attractive. Self-love is tricky because no matter how emotionally stable and secure you feel, you will always have insecurities that pop up every now and then.

If our insecurities involve the way we look, we may develop an obsession with losing weight, for example. But even when we lose weight, those insecurities are still there unless we heal them from within. If we choose to lose weight to attract a partner, losing weight will not make us happier. Therefore, it is often very difficult to lose weight because our motivation to lose it is decreased by twisted expectations.

Insecurities can take many forms and can distort our reality. Someone may see us as unimaginably beautiful, but we don't see it because there is always an impossible standard we strive to achieve. This distorts our reality and causes us unnecessary pain, such as writing someone off due to our own insecurities.

When we are insecure, we often settle for people who do not treat us well because we feel we can't do better. This is also due to our lack of self-worth; if we believe we deserve better, we will not allow ourselves to be treated badly.

This is not a dig at those who have self-worth issues. We all struggle when it comes to who we are and what we can offer in a relationship. What is most important is not what we look like but what we can offer emotionally.

Navigating the Dating World after a Divorce

After a significant relationship ends, we need to start fresh. If we want to experience marriage again, we must know what we want and not settle. By figuring out who we are and knowing what type of relationship we want to be in, we will be much happier and much better matched. Online dating has become so prevalent today that it is difficult to find someone who hasn't been on at least one of the online dating apps. It is rare to find someone organically.

Organic relationships are relationships that develop naturally and may start as friends. These relationships allow the two people involved to get to know each other more authentically. There is no pressure to act differently because it is already assumed that they are not interested in the other person. Eventually, one might develop feelings for the other in a more authentic way that is not based on an online picture or profile but rather on who they are as a person.

The problem with this is that when one friend develops feelings, they are afraid to express their feelings. The fear of rejection and embarrassment often prevents people from expressing their true feelings, but there is nothing embarrassing about confessing how we feel, even if those feelings are not reciprocated. However, if our feelings are not reciprocated, and it affects the friendship negatively, we must move on to avoid more hurt and confusion.

It is extremely important to be honest and upfront in any relationship. Sometimes honesty is hard, and we are afraid. We may want more in a relationship but are too afraid that the other doesn't feel the same. And because we don't want to lose what we currently have, we feel stuck and afraid and continue with the relationship. But this is never a healthy place to be. If we continue like this, things will never change, and eventually, the relationship might end because the other might feel the same but never have the courage to express themselves either. It is important to always express ourselves in relationships, no matter what. If a relationship is meant for you, it will sustain any uncomfortable conversations.

Yes, change can be scary, but it is also necessary so that we continue to evolve. We are not meant to stay the same. By staying with someone who does not fulfill our needs, we may be depriving ourselves of true happiness.

But how do we get to the point where we are okay with change? We need to accept the possibility of things not going our way. We must be emotionally mature to understand that both people in the relationship are not in the same phase of life or want the same things. There could be a variety of things that could affect relationships, such as location, work, and even children. These factors may affect a decision to be with someone, but if it's serious, these factors play no part in the decision.

Understanding Who We Are, What We Want in a Relationship, What to Look Out For, and Having the Courage to Express Our Wants in a Relationship to a Potential Partner

Understanding who we are and having independence is important. The idea that we need someone to "complete" us is skewed; however, most of us still approach relationships by looking for someone to make us whole. For example, if we lack spontaneity, we look for it in others. This is not to say that successful couples are the same. However, it's important not to pretend to be someone else in a relationship because we risk losing ourselves if we do.

What if we fall in love almost instantly? We can have an instant connection with someone but be afraid to express how we feel because falling in love quickly is not socially acceptable. The problem is the constant battle between our heads and hearts. Our mind is on the more logical side. It protects us from certain undesirable outcomes, but it doesn't consider that without risk, there is no reward. That means that many opportunities are lost if we only follow our heads.

So, what do we do? The first thing we must do is know what you want. Do we want a relationship, or do we want something casual? Are we willing to give up on a connection if the couple doesn't want the same thing? We must be honest. A relationship will not work if we want something long-term and the other is looking for something more casual. Anyone in this situation is at risk of being hurt or hurting someone else. And that is not fair.

What if we don't know what we want? It is important to know what we want, and if we think we want something casual, but it turns into something more, it is important to communicate this and be prepared for the connection to end if they decide that it isn't what they want. This can be hard, especially if we've developed significant feelings for them. But if we don't communicate, we risk getting hurt even more in the long run.

On the other hand, if we want a casual relationship but the other expresses they want more, it's important to be honest and not lead them on. Unfortunately, this happens a lot because we don't want to lose the other. However, this may cause distrust.

But what if this person is the real deal? What if this person wants everything we want? We will never know unless we trust them, but how? This is where we must follow our heart and gut. What do they tell us? This is scary because it's hard to listen to our intuition. However, what is the worst that can happen? If we decide to go for it and this person shows signs of inauthenticity, we can end the relationship. We are never obligated to pursue a connection, but it's a problem most of us have. We feel we must be nice or give excuses for other people's behaviour. And maybe the excuses are warranted, but sometimes they are red flags. We feel this obligation out of loyalty and fear of hurting people's feelings. However, honesty and communication are important aspects of any relationship. If the other does not know how we feel, it will always cause disruption and confusion.

How Mental Conditioning Affects Us and the Unhappiness That Follows

Our lives can turn out in many ways depending on our environment and emotional upbringing. We have already discussed how detrimental it is for children to lack emotional support from their parents and how teachers and professors can determine our worth regarding our intelligence and ability to get a job.

But let's dig deeper into how certain experiences growing up can affect our minds and how we behave as adults. A child's seemingly innocent act can have detrimental results as an adult if it's not appropriately processed. But how can we see these acts or be aware of them when the child or adult acts "normal" according to societal standards? How do we as adults justify these acts that happened to us as children?

So many of us hide a part of ourselves from other people that we don't want to be seen. We act in morally acceptable ways while holding back our desires to say what we mean or do what we want when a person acts badly toward us. We use the guise of being the bigger person because we know that resorting to violence would have terrible consequences. But what about the people who do not have inhibitions and do not care about consequences because they were treated badly and can't take it anymore? We hear it all the time in many movie troupes. The one who was bullied takes out their revenge on the bully.

Often the bullied seem quiet, submissive, and unsuspecting of committing a crime, but the inverse can happen, and they end up committing crimes and harming others because they did not receive support or feel unloved. However, they are not necessarily always bad people.

How do seemingly good people turn into bad people? How does one commit a crime so despicable? What is the psychology behind criminal behaviour, and can it be prevented or understood? Can we look past the mask, see the person behind the crime, and use compassion instead of persecution? Is it possible to forgive a person whose criminal behaviour destroyed our family? Can we prevent criminal acts from happening if we can understand and change the environment of the people that are most likely to commit these crimes? Can we understand how punishment and isolation can affect how a person's mental state can turn deadly? Can we teach and practice compassion to connect emotionally to people where the need to harm and commit crimes is no longer felt needed? Can we lose the stigma of people who are mentally ill or assume that these people are bad and that nothing can help them and that they will always be bad people? Can we understand and accept the idea of criminal reform?

CHAPTER 15

Parental Separation, Religious Upbringing, Abuse, and the Consequences That Follow

One of the most overlooked incidences in a child's life that could cause them to disconnect from feeling proper emotional connections is toxic parental relationships. In these instances, parental separation and divorce are necessary. But even though it is necessary, children must understand why.

Children may experience the separation or divorce differently through different perspectives based on the parent they are closest to or what each parent is telling them. Based on the level of understanding the child has, they may view a particular parent's perspective as more truthful than the other's, and this may cause parental alienation.

How Parents' Behaviour During a Divorce Can Affect Their Children

When parents who divorce or separate do not get along, it often hurts the children the most, especially when they believe one parent is bad because the other told them so. This is why it is not a good idea to speak poorly about each other to children. Children are especially impressionable; they may want to have the other parent like them or get special privileges if they side with one parent over the other. This can also be seen as manipulation or bribery.

A step further would be that children become afraid of one parent because of what the other tells them. This can have very dangerous consequences and cause psychological harm, such as feelings of being unloved, abandonment, and not being good enough. This can greatly affect children as they grow up in the way they form relationships, how worthy they feel in relationships, or simply mirroring the relationship they saw growing up.

As discussed, there are benefits to parents separating and divorcing to find a better and more loving connection. However, behaviours during a separation and divorce can affect how the children involved cope with their new living situations. When there are issues with child custody, one parent is often uncooperative or hostile.

This is difficult because this is often a move of control rather than in the children's best interest. Sometimes children are used as pawns in family court, which becomes an issue of parental alienation. Children can become traumatized, thinking one parent doesn't care about them or is not fighting to see them when the truth is that the parent does not have any control over the situation.

Sometimes parents fight for full custody, but the societal standards often favour the mother in these situations.

How Abuse Can Affect Emotional Connections with Parents, Partners, and Peers

A child who did not have a healthy upbringing and witnessed abuse may learn how to be abused or to be the abuser. It is very common to be emotionally and mentally abused and not know it because of the level of social acceptance. For generations, this has affected our ability to form loving connections. As discussed, there are many reasons why children become sad or distant or that they have no joy or excitement in their life. They may have little to no friends or do not have the courage to approach a child their age to make friends because they have been broken down so much by verbal abuse by their parents telling them that they don't love them and that no one else will love them or that they will always be by themselves so they should get used to it. This could be why we grow up with no friends or put any effort into making any friends. We might take every comment that a person says as a personal attack because we can only hear the negative when people talk about us. We might not believe a compliment when someone compliments us because we have been used so much that we associate a compliment with someone wanting something from us. We might have difficulty in romantic relationships because we have trouble knowing our worth as a human being because of how we were treated as children. As we know, it is almost impossible to form a loving connection to someone else if we don't value ourselves, and this results in partners pulling away from each other.

How Parents Can Project Their Own Fears About Potential Sexual Abuse to Their Children

No one should be in constant fear of being sexually abused, yet this is a parent's number one fear. Parents can warn their children and teach them acceptable and unacceptable behaviours, but they must be aware that they don't create distrust in their children. We cannot live in constant fear; we must be able to trust others but also assess potentially dangerous situations. Using our judgement is key.

Physical and Sexual Abuse by Parents

If a parent was physically abusive and nothing was done about the abuse, children may learn that this type of behaviour is normal, and this is how they should act. The same can be said for sexual abuse. If children are victims of sexual abuse and are told it is normal, it can confuse them. They may not know the devastating consequences it may have on someone, and depending on their understanding of abuse and their ability to discuss their feelings to an adult without the fear of punishment, they may think it is okay to repeat the same behaviours. Therefore, explaining to children what has happened to them and that it is not normal is important.

How Physical and Sexual Abuse Can Contribute to a Criminal Mindset

When we hear about adult sexual offenders, we are often not surprised when we find out that they were sexually abused as children or had a traumatic experience. This is not to say that every child or person who has experienced sexual abuse will become an abuser. In many cases, a child or person will take the opposite approach and become an advocate against it. Whatever road each of these individuals takes depends on the deep level of emotional trauma or the emotional connections given to them when the trauma took place.

A child who experienced deep emotional trauma that scarred their worth as a human being and received no love and support from anyone their entire life will not have the same emotional connection to other human beings because they associate human beings with the only people in their life that hurt them. They turn off their emotions as a defence mechanism to make themselves not hurt anymore. This is a very dangerous mindset to be in but also very sad. These are the individuals who do to others what was done to them or want others to hurt the way they hurt. These individuals often prey on people that have what they want and what they feel like they could never have.

Dealing with Sexual Abuse Trauma in Relationships

If we do not feel a strong emotional connection to someone, we may pull back sexually or may not want to be sexually intimate. When someone is sexually abused, they may react differently to sexual acts. They may wish to connect more on an emotional level because sexual intimacy is still traumatic for them, and without communicating it to their partner, it can cause unhealthy feelings. Therefore, it is important for someone who has been sexually abused to understand their worth. Most who have been sexually abused believe their partner will only love them for what they can bring to the relationship sexually. This is especially dangerous when their partner takes advantage of them. Furthermore, if someone was sexually abused, they may become more sexually active at a young age and believe that to be liked, they had to perform sexual acts.

On the other hand, some of those who have been sexually abused may decide that they do not want to be objectified and never want that to happen to them again. This may cause them to refrain from all sexual acts and feel very uncomfortable with even the thought of sexual intercourse.

These individuals may flinch at having a partner and may question whether someone is interested in them for the right reasons.

Self-Esteem Issues from Trauma

This kind of trauma can also cause problems with one's self-esteem or weight gain. Some who have been sexually abused might believe it happened to them because they looked a certain way, so they try to make themselves undesirable. People underestimate the correlation between sexual abuse and weight gain. It is common for someone who was sexually abused to develop a food addiction, especially at a young age. This is because they lack control in their lives, so the only way they can control some part of their lives is to control how much they eat. Because of this, food becomes a comfort to them, much like an addiction to drugs. However, this can also go the other way where those who have been sexually abused will restrict food. Often they view this as self-punishment for what happened to them.

Sometimes the sexually abused can get triggered by certain words or actions from a loving partner, which can cause intimacy issues, such as feeling uncomfortable being sexual or having their partner see them naked or having their partner comment on how sexually turned on they might feel. This can be extremely uncomfortable and remind them of their abuse.

If the sexually abused were young when their sexual abuse happened, their parents might have told them it was wrong. However, the sexually abused might have wrongly interpreted that to mean all sex is wrong and thus have difficulty processing their sexuality into adulthood. We are all sexual beings, but some of us are too ashamed to express it in a healthy way. Instead, we suppress it and pretend it doesn't exist because we are too embarrassed to talk about it. This often goes hand in hand with being told that we should be ashamed of our bodies.

How Religion Affects Relationships and Sexuality

How children are raised can impact their intimate relationships. They can model them after their parents or religious upbringing.

Some religions use control and fear to keep their followers compliant, stating the difference between right and wrong. However, no one nor any religion should have a set of rules that anyone must follow under the stipulation that they are bad and sinful if they do not obey these rules.

Many religions consider homosexuality to be a sin, which is extremely hypocritical, considering that most religions preach love, tolerance, and acceptance.

Being raised in a religious household comes with feeling controlled. Many religions consider sexual relationships and moving in together before marriage to be sinful. When children are told that it is wrong to have sexual thoughts, they begin to suppress or hide them, and this is where sexual insecurities are formed. Furthermore, those raised in religious households are shamed into believing anything that goes against their religious beliefs. Religions use words like "master," "worship," and "obey." This is wrong. Look at these words closely. What is a master? A master is someone who is in control of others. If we call someone our master, we take away any control we might have over ourselves and our decisions. The same goes for worshiping and obeying. Religions often tell us to worship and obey our master. What does this mean? That we cannot distinguish what is right and wrong on our own? We must obey our master? This is how cults are formed. In cults, there is often someone in charge of a large majority of people. These people are promised something they want or value. They are told that to get it, they must obey their leader; they must do what their leader tells them and teach others to obey them as well. Cult leaders will often instil fear into those who do not think like them.

Just like our information is often controlled by the media, religious practices and teachings are often controlled by those providing the information. It's important to remember that children can be manipulated and want praise and affection so much that they will grow up believing everything their family and religion tell them.

CHAPTER 16

How Unhappiness Can Affect Future Behaviour and Coping Mechanisms

By the time we reach adulthood, many of us have had many experiences that significantly impacted us. We may have developed self-esteem issues because we compared ourselves to others, such as our peers or influencers and others we follow on social media. Our lives may look dull and meaningless because we are unhappy in our chosen careers, or we're stuck in loveless marriages we can't leave.

Bringing light again to topics in earlier chapters is to help emphasize and remind us of how these experiences have consequences and how when we perceive our life negatively can affect our mental and emotional health in the present. Sometimes how we deal with these consequences is through coping mechanisms. What happens to us when we are constantly unhappy and miserable? What happens when we suppress our emotions so much that we cannot be ourselves? What kind of undesirable consequences occur if our seemingly normal lives take a turn we don't expect?

When we live unwelcome experiences, we use those experiences to project them onto others.

Coping mechanisms are a form of escape. They are a way to repress memories and feelings about the abuse we endured, allowing us to project a seemingly normal demeanour while we are a complete mess on the inside.

Forms of coping mechanisms can present themselves as various addictions. When we think of addictions, we often think about drugs and alcohol. However, this is not always the case, even though they are the addictions that are commonly recognized and taken seriously.

Addictions and Coping Mechanisms

Addictions can be in the form of anything that impedes our day-to-day lives, including scrolling through social media, watching television, shopping, and eating. We all joke about shopping addictions, but sometimes they go deeper. There are always extremes to every addiction.

With trauma, we often feel comfort in the stuff we know and the stuff we can control. A person with a hoarding problem may feel in control of their life by holding onto as many things as possible, even if that feeling is temporary. The same goes for someone with a shopping problem. These and other addictions are just coping mechanisms for something much deeper.

However, the problem with any addiction is that when we stop, we realize what we've done, making us feel even worse.

Rehab for Addictions

Another issue is that too much emphasis is placed on rehab when addiction happens. However, when someone is sent to rehab unwillingly, it doesn't work because we can't force someone to get better. They need to want to get better for themselves. This is why when a person goes to rehab willingly, they have more success with the program because they are more inclined to believe the doctors are there to help.

Sometimes addictions are diagnosed alongside mental illness, such as depression, and drugs are prescribed. Unfortunately, this happens a lot. But what if it was possible to dig deeper and help individuals cope with their addictions by looking to the root of the problem? When someone recognizes their addiction and recognizes that it is nothing to be ashamed of, they have much more success in getting better and moving past their addiction. And when we confront the trauma we've experienced that caused the addiction or the coping mechanism in the first place, we can heal.

When Trauma and Coping Mechanisms Affect Others

When parents can't take care of their children, have problems taking care of their children due to addictions, or their parenting styles do not coincide with what society views as acceptable, their children are most likely taken away. This causes strong emotional discomfort to the children and parents alike. Sometimes there is abuse involved, so there is a deeper issue to handle, but more often, when a child is taken away, it is because of neglect.

Neglect often happens when parents are dealing with addictions and difficult emotions. Many parents become villainized and criminalized because of their addictions, and instead of helping parents get better, the system takes their children away as a form of punishment that further evokes unpleasant emotions in them.

When children are taken away, they often do not want to leave. They are tested and prodded for mental illness and are often put in foster homes. Foster children are often seen or stereotyped as damaged. They are often stigmatized as having problems, whether they be behavioural or developmental. This takes a toll on those who are placed in foster care as they are often told by those taking care of them that their behaviour is not normal. Now, these children must deal with the stigma and judgement that comes with living in a foster home.

As a result, many foster children who age out of the system are not healed from the trauma, stigma, and judgement. They are left to figure everything out for themselves, and most do not know what to do or how to cope. They feel rejected, alone, and unsupported.

On the other hand, some foster children heal from their experiences and manage to cope with them in a healthy way, leading them to have successful futures. The sad part of this, however, is that when they tell their success story to others, they are met with people who say they were "lucky" or the "odd one" or that someone must have helped them along the way, which takes away their power. Only we can heal our personal trauma, not external forces.

Sexual Abuse and Coping Mechanisms

Children who have been sexually abused may be confused about what is normal and abnormal behaviour. They may be manipulated and told by their abusers that the abuse is normal. If sexual abuse goes on for years and it is not found out, children may grow up to think it's normal and repeat the same behaviour. Sadly, those who do repeat this behaviour believe they are doing what they believe is normal and don't understand they are hurting others.

However, when they realize that sexual abuse is not normal and that what happened to them was wrong, they must deal with the aftermath of their understanding of their abuse.

Sexual abuse is a serious crime and sad as well because often, those who commit these crimes are victims themselves who never received help.

Sometimes when a person is so abused that the abuse has become a part of them, they begin to normalize it to cope with it and make it less traumatic. This is why many children who are kidnapped often become attached to their abusers, or when they are manipulated and abused enough, they convince themselves they are not being abused and that they have chosen the abuse. When the abused face their fears and come to terms with the reality of their abuse, it feels traumatizing because they have finally come to the realization that their life and free will were taken from them. Therefore, it is sometimes easier to live with the delusion that the abuse never happened. However, these are merely coping mechanisms.

Relationships and Coping Mechanisms

This can also be the case for being in a bad relationship or a bad marriage. Sometimes when we want something so bad, like kids and a marriage, we overlook certain red flags. We tell ourselves that these behaviours are okay and that we are just being picky or that we should lower our standards when it comes to expectations for our partner. We have discussed earlier why some marriages and relationships fall apart. However, what we have not discussed is why women or men continue to stay in marriages and relationships when they are being abused or mistreated.

We tell ourselves that there is nothing wrong and that we are ridiculous for feeling so angry over little things when it's no big deal to do it ourselves. We will often give excuses for our spouse when others notice it by saying things like "They do not normally talk to me like that" or "They are just having a bad day. Excuse their behaviour; they didn't mean to snap at me." Verbal and emotional abuse is not widely accepted as abuse that can yield damage, but it certainly does.

As a coping mechanism, the person in the marriage that is being verbally abused might pretend everything is okay to everyone around them, and to everyone's knowledge, they are happy. This person might convince themselves that they are happy when they are not. This coping mechanism keeps them stuck in a marriage that is not good for them, and they may become a different person to accommodate these numb feelings for the sake of the marriage. It is a mindset that is difficult to get out of, and many live their lives this way, never finding true happiness in a loving and caring relationship.

CHAPTER 17

Why Trauma and Coping with Trauma May Result in Undesirable Behaviour

A therapist's job is to make us aware of our feelings and make us feel comfortable with expressing how we feel in a safe and non-judgemental space. However, it is our own ability to take those feelings and transform them into something healing.

People often push therapy as a quick fix to heal our trauma, but it is only a tool; only we have the power to heal ourselves. If someone feels forced into therapy, the therapy will be meaningless. The problem is when people do not get their feelings validated, they will often believe that they are bad and will act accordingly, sometimes going as far as committing crimes. However, this all depends on one's emotional maturity and ability to assess their feelings and heal them properly. Sometimes children who were taught to listen and obey during childhood act out as adults when their parents no longer control them. In extreme instances, these crimes can involve something as terrible as taking another person's life or taking advantage of others forcefully. When this occurs, others will say the bad behaviour is out of character and will be shocked because, on the surface, the person who committed the crime seemed perfectly well-behaved and always followed the rules.

These outbursts can cause serious harm to others, and there must be consequences for them, but if we understand why these crimes occurred, we can help those who committed the crimes heal from the trauma and potentially become less dangerous.

If it is a small crime, the trauma is easier to heal if the person wants to heal. Sometimes it is just as easy as understanding why the outburst happened and how it came to be. Other times the criminal is stubborn and does not want any help, and is very distrustful because of the lack of support in their life.

The criminals that commit the more terrible crimes are more difficult to handle. This has become a controversial topic. Yes, every crime should have consequences, but when we look at the person who committed the crime, we need to ask why they did it. This is why many prisoners should have access to therapists.

Having Compassion for Criminals

This becomes an issue of compassion. How much compassion can we have for a person who took another person's life, especially if it was someone we loved? We would most likely want the most punishable sentence by law. It is unlikely that we would see it otherwise. However, if we understood the motives behind the crime, could we possibly forgive them? Most will say no, but some will say yes.

The Correlation Between Control and Choice That Stems from Our Childhood

Often the criminals won't even know why they committed the crime. What they often say is that they couldn't control themselves. And if the crime was premeditated, they might say they had no choice. Let's take a good look at this more closely. Saying "I had no choice" might go as far back as their childhood, where they grew up feeling they had no choice in any decision of their lives. This happens in situations where we don't know why we do things because we are often on autopilot to survive.

The way we process our feelings as children influences how well-balanced we are as adults. Often when we have no way to process our feelings or when we feel there is no way out and no one cares, we take drastic measures to have our voices heard, even if it is just through our actions. Sometimes this takes the form of fetishes, which are often kept secret. They call it our dark side for a reason, as even our closest friends and family don't know about them.

If we are aware of how we talk to children and encourage them to freely be themselves and express themselves, maybe they wouldn't rebel.

If we told our children that they do not need to believe what we believe or abide by our religious standards, perhaps they would properly process their feelings and be the best versions of themselves. What if we released ourselves from the societal expectations that we must live a certain way? Only then can our minds be free from societal thinking.

Allowing our children to have feelings can prevent childhood trauma and prevent this cycle of abuse. Not controlling everything in their lives can allow them to think and take care of themselves.

We should normalize communicating our feelings. We should be able to recognize those with coping mechanisms and support them, not punish them. We can heal subconscious trauma by talking about it and unleashing it.

We should spread compassion and kindness and not hate so that we can help with the unconscious beliefs people have. No one is perfect but trying to be better is better than being hateful.

How We Can Break Free from This Mindset and Live the Life We Were Meant to Have

What if we could turn our lives around? What if we looked at our lives and asked ourselves if we were happy? Do we have the life we pictured having as children? If yes, that's wonderful; however, I assume most of us said no. We may be stuck in a relationship or marriage that doesn't fulfil us or we may be stuck in a job that drains our mental and physical energy every day. We may feel inadequate and hopeless in navigating our lives in a more positive and happier manner. But what if we could change all that?

Why are we stuck with these feelings of hopelessness and lack of control? Why do we feel the inability to change our lives for the better? Why do we have negative feelings towards others and their circumstances? Why do we feel inferior to others and act in ways we are ashamed of? Is it just easier to follow the crowd or more fulfilling to set our own path away from the expectations that others set on us and the expectations we set on ourselves? Can we break free from societal thinking and ways of doing things and start doing things our own way? Are we willing to let go and give up the high standards we set for ourselves without judgement or fear of judgement from others?

How can we change? How can we reprogram our minds to break the chains that were placed on us? What stops us from changing everything in our lives, and what will it take us to truly do what we want to do? Is money worth all the unhappiness that comes with earning it? Can we break the pull that money has on us as a societal standard and be happy doing what we love to do and loving life every day but making less money? Do we need money to be happy? Or is that just what we have been taught to believe? Once we break free from this mindset, true happiness will follow.

CHAPTER 18

Breaking Down the Standards That Shaped Us

Those who break or go against societal standards are viewed as disrespectful and "wrong" by those who comply and blindly do what they are told. Unfortunately, they are the loudest, but that doesn't make them right.

People often lead with logic and information, but sometimes the information we are given can be misleading. The best thing we can do is trust our gut. However, this can sometimes be confused with nerves or worries about the unfamiliar. However, if we are inclined to do something even though it's risky and feels uncomfortable, we should follow our intuition. Our intuition can lead us to something new and get us out of our comfort zones.

When we get out of the mindset that we need to follow societal standards to be successful or can't make money and be successful doing something we love, we will find what makes us happy and successful.

Being Brave to Break Apart from the Life We Have Always Known

There will always be someone or some institution telling us how to think and behave and what is right and wrong, and if we fall out of line, there will be consequences. Consequences are important, but at what cost? We are so afraid of consequences because we were raised to be afraid. We have difficulty standing up for things against the norm because we risk being segregated and called misinformed or laughed at just because we question the information presented to us.

This may be confusing because most people won't take the time to do the research and get both sides of every story. It's important to always get both sides to each story and try not to trust the media too much or the people reporting on it. Most of the time, the media or reporters will report on the popular opinion of the public and run with it. This is equivalent to starting a rumour about someone else, getting many people to believe it, and provoking a specific emotion based on that rumour when there could be false aspects. This is mostly done with people in the public eye. Some people make a living off reporting these rumours and further perpetuating hate under the guise of keeping people accountable.

Thinking Critically about How We Act and How to Change

Our society has become a cesspool of people who feel they have the right to dictate how other people want to live their lives. Sometimes these people can do no right. If they show off where they live, they are bragging or if they talk about how sad they are, they are scrutinized for being sad because of how seemingly perfect their lives are. Also, people who don't have what these people have will often become so jealous that they put down how this person makes their money and how they spend it. We often get so involved in other peoples' lives that we make assumptions about them.

We are social creatures. When we have an opinion about something, and someone has the same opinion, we often solidify that opinion as though someone else validating it makes it more authentic. This will often pull people together as there are shared interests. However, sometimes these opinions are not authentic, and we only agree because we don't want to start a fight, we don't want to offend anyone, or we want others to like us.

When we think critically, we may begin to rethink everything we have ever been told. Is this the truth, or was there more to the story? Why did we get so extremely upset over what someone else told us? This may be because the person that told us meant a lot to us and their pain upset us, so we decided to take matters into our own hands and get justice. We all make mistakes but to blindly attack someone on behalf of another person, especially when we do not know the full story, can make us a contributor to targeted harassment. However, most of us do not want to be a part of this. We want to stand up for the people we love, correct? Well, this applies to everyone. We have people on both ends of every situation, and whether they are right or wrong, both sides need to be heard.

Often the reason we think a certain way is because that is what we are told to think. Since childhood, we've been manipulated to think a certain way, and if we don't, we get punished.

Freeing Our Minds from the Information We Grew Up With

When we have an opinion but are unsure about it, and then someone else validates our opinion, we often consider it a fact even though it might be false. This can also be a bonding experience, and often, what happens is that we become so enthralled in this bonding experience that we want to continue it. We will then find other things to have in common. However, this can only last for so long because there will be something that you both might disagree on and often sometimes, that will tear the friendship apart if you are so used to thinking and believing the same way.

Because of the nature of our fast-paced lives, do we ever just sit with ourselves and think about who we are or want to be? We often ask ourselves these questions when something falls apart, and we are left to pick up the pieces. The question we must then ask ourselves is what do we want to keep from our past, and what do we want to change?

Before our parents and society told us who we were supposed to be, who were we? Why did we not continue doing what made us happy? Would we still want to do that now? Questions like this will spark a new curiosity in life and a new passion in ourselves.

We must think deeply about what makes us happy. What can we do to make ourselves happy? How can we make this happen? What goals can we set to accomplish this? Even though things may seem slow, we should enjoy the process. Some of us may want to learn something new or start a new project. Some may feel a new zest for life and feel energized. There is often freedom that comes with starting something new.

Once we start to think critically, we realize how often we've blindly believed things in the past. Once we are more aware of this, we can look at both sides of a situation with no bias and open our eyes to what is being presented to us in the media, television, and movies.

How much of what we believe is based on someone telling us what to think and how to think? We see this happening all around us, and this can sometimes lead to being on the wrong side of justice because we are blind to the other side. Furthermore, the more this happens, the more we cannot admit we were wrong. We have a hard time admitting to ourselves that what we did or thought was wrong, and instead of admitting that we are stubborn, we will fight tooth and nail to prove we were right the whole time. This often happens when we do not have a lot of emotional intelligence to properly assess a situation and feel confident in ourselves to admit our wrongdoings.

Relearning Information from a Different Perspective

Just like what we have learned in other chapters, the problem with information is that with learning, some information becomes outdated. However, most people take old information as absolute fact without the possibility of improvement. There should always be different ways of looking at information. There is never a one size fits all type of situation.

Herein lies the problem: many believe that one solution fits everyone because they are afraid of change and never want to get out of their comfort zone. They will continue to blindly believe what they have been told to believe their entire lives. These are usually the people who look for others for information and lack control in their lives.

When we constantly look for outside validation and information, we never allow ourselves the ability to look at the information from an outside perspective. Only when professionals go against the grain are new ideas and thoughts about a subject formed. Often when this happens, it is not well received because it goes against the normal expectations and societal standards. We only accept it when new information comes out that supports our existing beliefs. If we went with any new conflicting information, we would be questioning our whole belief system, which would put us outside our comfort zones. Most of us accept the information presented to us because that is what we have always been taught.

This often happens when we start breaking down the learning standards we were taught in our profession. To think for ourselves, we need to break down the learning and standards that were taught to us and question their validity. So how do we know what information is true? We must look inside ourselves to find the answer. Who are we, and what do we believe? This may change us completely because we will become people who are no longer shaped by others and society. We may lose ourselves, but we may also open ourselves up to the very different possibilities of information. This is a clean slate to becoming a more authentic person. Being a more authentic person is scary, but we must trust ourselves. No one should shape our lives but us.

When you reshape your thinking, you realize how misinformed you once were. However, most people around you will still believe the old information, but it's important to be tolerant as you were once blindly unaware also.

CHAPTER 19

Why Can't We Do and Say the Things We Want Without Feeling Judged?

Why is it difficult for us to feel in the moment what we want to do or when we see it we call it weird or embarrassing? If we want to fun and play with our children often people will stop and not want to continue this because they are self conscious, or they think that the person around them will judge then as being weird.

Why Our Feelings of Being Weird and Judged Stem from Our Childhood. We Are Taught Not to Say What We Want to Say for Fear of Hurting Other People's Feelings

Why are we teaching our children not to be goofy and make funny faces and say what they want to say when other people are around? Children are the most honest people; they say what is on their minds and ask questions when they do not know how certain things work and what to do. This is often followed by parents telling them to be quiet because what they said was inappropriate. This is called having no filter.

However, children are not badly intentioned; they simply say what is on their minds and will, for the most part, answer questions honestly. A child will lie only when they are afraid to get into trouble. So, if we have this trust in children, why don't we have this trust in adults when they tell us how they feel?

Feeling like People Are Lying to Us Because They Are Afraid to Hurt Our Feelings

Why do we always accuse people of lying or accuse them of having an alternative motive when it comes to information? Why do we always feel manipulated? Maybe if we were more honest with people and did not try to manipulate them in a roundabout way, our communication would be better, and we would not have to question each other.

But some adults do not trust children and believe that children are intentional and manipulative when they say things. These adults have serious trust issues.

Trust Issues in Adulthood

Can we get to the point where it becomes normal to want to help someone without thinking you are looking for something in return? On the other hand, can we get to the point where we want to help someone and not think about what we can get out of it?

This type of transactional exchange is why we have difficulty trusting people and their intentions to help us. There is nothing worse than helping someone and that person taking advantage of your generosity. Unfortunately, this breaks your trust in helping someone that might need and appreciate it because you have had a bad experience. Unfortunately, this happens all the time, and it is unfortunate because it prevents other people from getting the help they need.

We want to help others but are often stopped by the thought of being taken advantage of. On the other hand, everyone wants to feel appreciated, but if you are only doing something for someone because you want them to repay you, you are not the nice person you present yourself to be.

This is where people have difficulty accepting help because often that help comes with strings attached. Also, look out for those who do something nice and then tell many people about it. This is because they crave validation. A person who truly wants to help won't want recognition for it.

CHAPTER 20

Changing How We Look at Money and Career and Having the Courage to Follow Our Dreams

Taking the initial step to do something you want to do is the first step to finally doing what you want. Getting out of the mindset that you must have a mainstream job to be successful is the first step to finding what you want to do. Often, we are so enthralled by school and what people tell us to do that we often do not have an answer when we are asked what we enjoy. Tying into the previous chapter, we discussed how often young adults are pushed into further education and a career that they do not like because of the need for security and societal acceptance. However, as an adult unhappy in their current state of employment, we may start to view those things differently. Figuring out what we want to do and coming up with a plan to make the change as smooth as possible is important. However, this is often met with criticism because doing what we love requires money. But at what cost? If we see ourselves in a specific lifestyle with a nice house and nice things, at what cost do we sacrifice our time for that lifestyle? This is where we get stuck. We grow up with movies and television that tell us to value material things, but why do we want those things? Do we value them as much as we think, or do we value them because we are told to value them?

Realizing How Much Other People's Perspectives about Our Success Affects How We View Success Ourselves

As we change our thinking about career expectations and success, our minds will view these things differently. We will start to think critically and ask ourselves, "How much of what we want is related to how much we want to be liked and perceived by others?? Do we want the fancy car because we value it, or do we want it because we want others to envy us? Would a luxury car mean the same to us if no one saw it?

If the answer is no, let's examine it further. If that luxury car only means something of value to us because others can see it, why do you put so much time and money into it? If we only buy luxury vehicles to impress others, why do we value the opinions of others more than time away from our family at work?

Let's look deeper at that concept. A typical workweek is eight hours a day, five days per week. When we get home, we often want to relax. We go to work so that we can come home to a nice house that we hardly get to spend time in and drive a car that we hardly get to use. We pay someone else to take care of our children that we don't get to raise. And all of this because we want to impress others.

These are acceptable societal standards, but we often wonder why this is acceptable when we break it down. How are we okay working at a job we barely like to make money for items we don't need to be happy to impress people we don't like? Of course, some love their jobs, and the luxury car and house are things they don't need to show off to others but value; this is what we should all strive for.

But sometimes we don't have that. Sometimes we realize that we don't need all of that, that we are happy without money, our life, and that we don't value what other people value. It is important to realize everyone is different.

The Difference Between Money and Happiness

Some people are happy with the simple life they create as long as they do something they love. These are sometimes the people that give up high-demanding corporate jobs. Often this is because they are unhappy with their life in the corporate job, and they choose to do something they love even without the stability they once had.

This may be outrageous for some to think about, but money isn't everything. We are told by society to chase the money to get the bigger house, the fancier car, and have the nicest things, but in the end, is it worth it?

What if we looked at things differently? What if we valued things differently? Would we still want the same things we want now? If we look at what we want right now, we might say we want a nice house, a nice car, and a tropical vacation. But if we imagine having them already, what made us want them so badly? It could be that we associate these things with a level of success. But what if these things didn't define success?

How Celebrities Affect How We View Success and Happiness

As mentioned in previous chapters, material things have become status symbols of success rather than something we want. At the end of the day, a small house has the same function as a large house, and a normal car still has the same function as a luxury one. But why do we value one more than the other?

We often value what we don't have. We see celebrities in their fancy houses, and we wish we had what they have. Our society glamorizes material things in magazines and movies. But what we don't see is the hard work and the sacrifice behind attaining these things. Often celebrities live in movie trailers and sacrifice spending time with their family and children. We don't see how hard they are pushed and how have no choice in their working conditions.

Yet this is what we idolize as fans. The sacrifice of time over money is often not understood in the public eye because society values money so much. We compare our lives to others who have money, saying we wish we were them. But when we start to change our mind about what constitutes success and wealth, then we stop comparing ourselves to others and people in the public eye.

Being Grateful for What We Have

However, we must remember to look at our lives and be grateful for what we have. Do we have a roof over our heads? Can we pay our bills? Do we have food? Do we have a family we love? These are the important things. Most of the time, we have it backwards; we focus on what we don't have.

This is how some families feel neglected or not good enough because we become so focused on material things that we do not look at the organic things we have in front of us. We choose to work late and spend time away from family and friends with the goal of pursuing something better. Often, we even see our families as a burden to us, spending unnecessary money on them when that money could go to other material things.

How Material Items and Success Can Affect Relationships and Marriages

This is also how marriages and families fall apart because we don't value them as something important. But why? Why would we ever value anything material over something we love? Our drive for status and success often takes over our lives until we reach a point that it is too late. Often when we reach this level of success, we have no one to share it with because we turned our back on everyone in the pursuit of success.

However, if we are doing what we love and not sacrificing our lives and the lives of those around us, we are doing it right. There are people out there who are extremely wealthy doing what they love. This is what everyone should strive for. This is what is important. This is success the right way.

Often when this happens, success follows. When we do what we love and are not attached to any outcome, our success is a bonus. This is the best way to view life.

CHAPTER 21

How Different Our Lives Would Be if We Did What We Loved/ Challenges with Being Authentic

When you decide to do what you want to do, and you do not care about monetary gain, success follows when you are least expecting it. This is what happens with many wealthy people.

Also, when money doesn't have a hold on you and you do not reach a high level of success, you will still be just as happy because your mindset is different.

You don't need money to be happy; you can still have a happy life because you are doing what you love.

Giving Up Wealth and Success for Pure Happiness

Not everything that seems happy and perfect on the outside is as happy and perfect on the inside. Someone out there could have all the riches in the world and would gladly give them up if it meant they could be happy.

But this is a difficult mindset to get into, especially with the amount of emphasis society has placed on the importance of money and material things. This is why you should take a deep look into why you want money and status. How do you see yourself when you have the money and status, and who is there with you?

How do you get there? How do you create something that makes you happy that you can see yourself doing for the rest of your life and not getting sick of it? However ridiculous it may seem to you right now, how much does doing it make you happy? For some, it is about learning something new, and for others, it is about continuing to practice something they love but don't have the time for anymore.

What about starting over and learning something you always wanted to learn without the goal of making money? Think about how you could be waking up every day wanting to work instead of dreading it like most of us do. The reality of having a job that you enjoy is that the less money-driven you are, the more wealth you will acquire, which is ironic.

Having the Courage to Do What You Love

Often when we make a drastic change in our lives and people do not understand, it can take courage to let those people go if they give us a hard time about our decisions. Remember to take control of your life; you do not work for others you. Stand firm and be happy with your decision to be free. This is the only way to reach your full potential and be truly happy. This can often hold people back when wanting to start something new because other people's opinions are often valuable.

This could be a very difficult thing to do if you have been controlled most of your life. Your parents may not agree with your current life path, especially when they expect you to enter a specific profession. This is also difficult if you have a spouse who does not agree with this change.

How Others May Affect Your Choice to Start a New Career

We have already discussed how marriages can end, but we have not discussed how marriages can end because of a career change or lack of security. Often this can break marriages up because there is no level of compromise and only a level of control. Again, if a spouse truly understands your passions and wishes, they will want to support and grow with you. If a spouse is not on the same page as you and the financial security scares them, then it should be a decision that both of you discuss. You will need to look at how much the relationship means to you to compromise your passions and dreams.

If you can't let go of your spouse because they mean more to you than your passion and dreams, choose them, but if you want to follow your passions and dreams and feel you would recent your spouse for making them choose, then choose your passions. You never want to feel like you made the wrong decision; it is unfair to yourself and your spouse to choose them when your marriage falls apart because of them. It is always important to have open communication regarding these things, even though it could be the most difficult decision to make.

People may disagree with this, but choosing your passions and dreams over your spouse may save you time with what is inevitable. What I mean is that when you choose your passions, you are becoming your more authentic self.

Challenges of Being Your Most Authentic Self

Being your most authentic self is being the happiest you can be. This is because you are finally breaking free from the mindset that you must be a completely different person than you are. We are never allowed to be just us. We are never given a chance to sit with our thoughts and feelings to figure out what we want. We always have someone or something telling us what we are and what we think about things.

We must question whether something is what we think or what we are supposed to think. Do I hate that person, or am I told to hate that person? Breaking down barriers can be a scary and difficult thing, but it is what it takes to become knowledgeable about the hold the world and society have on us. We might question our beliefs when this happens. We might have a personality crisis and not know who we are.

Becoming a More Authentic You

We are authentic when we believe what we truly believe and not what others believe. When we are more authentic and are not afraid to express our beliefs, a sense of freedom and authenticity takes over. This could be because we are morphing into the person we want to be.

If someone disagrees with us, we often pull away, thinking they are not on our side. However, debating is healthy. When we think differently, we can get along with those who do not think like us. Unfortunately, some refuse to be around anyone who may think differently. These people are often preaching tolerance, which is hypocritical because they do not tolerate other thought patterns aside from their own.

It is difficult to get out of the mindset that we must believe what others believe and that we must like what others like. How much of what we are told was told by someone else, etc.? How much of this information is controlled? Think about it.

CHAPTER 22

How Others' Opinions Affect Us and Navigating Inauthentic People

What is real and what is unreal, and how can we deal with those around us who do not view the world as we do? We will often question how we had managed to think another way for so long and what we can do to help others break free from the current mindset that the world has us in—the current mindset that prevents us from doing what we want and from being happy. The freedom to be and do what we want is endless, and when we break free from societal pressures and demands, it is so exhilarating.

This often happens when we stop caring what people think about us. Why do we care about others' opinions? Why does it matter?

Let's take a deeper look. We often live our lives in a way that pleases others. We don't want to offend someone, so we keep our opinions to ourselves, and we don't want to be embarrassed, so we don't try to do something, but why does it matter? Why do we care if others see our failure? Why do we compare ourselves to other people's success? Why does someone else's success lower our success?

Learning How to Be Unaffected When People Call Us Bad Names

These things do not make sense. If we know inside that we are a good person, and someone calls us a bad person, why does that affect us? It often affects us because we secretly feel it too.

Let's look at someone who is called a racist. If someone knows they are not a racist and someone else calls them a racist, they might say, "No, I'm not," and shrug it off. This is because they know that they have never said anything or done anything racist to constitute that comment. However, if they responded, "How dare they call me a racist! I am not a racist!" and spew other hurtful things to the other person and continue to get worked up about it. This could be because subconsciously, they feel there is some truth to that statement and their overtly aggressive reaction is them trying to overcome this feeling that they have inside them.

Our reactions to the world around us when we are not whole are difficult to manage. We look to others and project our insecurities onto them. We overcompensate what we feel we lack.

Hypocrisies of Name-Calling

A person with underlining racist tendencies will often project themselves as a defender of minorities and call other people racist when they fail to acknowledge their own racist tendencies. Often the people who speak the loudest are those who overly project themselves because of something they don't have or something they want.

This is a difficult pill to swallow. No one wants to hear that the loudest advocates are the biggest hypocrites. Once again, this is not the case with everyone. Those who are content with who they are and what they stand for and let their actions speak for them are not bothered. We see this all the time in society. Some choose to start fights and look for others to fight with. And then, in the same breath, they say they are fighting for something important only to make themselves look better. These are the individuals we must look out for because they are two-faced and will pretend they care. These people do everything they say they are against. They are hypocrites.

Struggling to Be Authentic Ourselves

Typically, authentic people do not need to be flashy with their good deeds or opinions. It is typically not a good sign when someone is overly nice because it means they are compensating for something. Many people do this but do not realize they are doing it. This is why it is difficult to find authentic friends and relationships. So why is it so hard to be authentic? We are often not authentic because we feel our authentic traits are undesirable. These are the traits that our surface self tries to compensate for. We may feel insecure or feel we are bad at something, so we compensate by saying we don't like it and that it's stupid and then bully or harass and make fun of those who are actually good at it.

All these behaviours are created by ignoring and shaming our true feelings. And why do we ignore and shame these feelings? We do this because we feel we must suppress our natural feelings and that if we were to express them, they would give us an undesirable outcome. We feel this way because society tells us we will get an undesirable outcome. We feel safe hiding our true emotions and acting in socially accepted ways because it is comfortable for us. It is difficult to break free from something that has always been done a certain way. But we must think about the possibilities of truly being ourselves and not caring what others and society think.

How Our Self-Esteem and Feelings Throughout Our Lives Prevent Us from Embracing Our Authentic Self and Gifts and Talents.

If we could access all the hidden feelings we've suppressed for so long and acknowledge them instead of feeling ashamed of them, we would become a different person—a more balanced, emotionally secure, and authentic person.

This may seem far-fetched to those who have difficulty expressing their feelings, but this is the first step. It is important to realize the feelings that do not match what we outwardly express. By doing so, we may realize that what we thought we liked, we don't, etc.

This is why we see many young adults putting their artistic talents aside because society doesn't deem the arts as a successful career. Often these people will settle and convince themselves that they were better off pursuing something more tangible because it offers more stability even though it doesn't make them happy. This is sad because these are the people who live their entire lives not expressing their talents. After all, society told them they were not good enough.

On the other hand, some choose to take the risk and follow their dreams. This is difficult for them because it often requires courage, but in the end, it's a rewarding way to live.

Having the Courage to Be Ourselves and Surround Ourselves with Authentic People

People who are one hundred percent authentic are constantly adapting and growing. However, they are whole. They are happy with themselves and are not bothered by others because they are happy and secure in themselves.

This seems like a difficult task for some, and it is, but it's not impossible. The most difficult part of reaching this stage is being aware that we are not acting in accordance with how we feel on the inside.

The second difficult task is to become aware that our feelings need to be properly processed and healed. To heal these feelings, we must accept and love them as parts of us. Only when we can look at our flaws and embrace them can we grow from them and love ourselves. This is by far the most difficult thing to do because the way most of us have lived our lives has been chosen and dictated by others. How we see beauty and appropriate behaviour and what constitutes success and intelligence have always been up to others and what society thinks.

However, when we reach this point in our journey, we realize that the hold others and society have on us means so little now, and we realize that what matters is what we think of ourselves and the way we view the world. When this happens, we have a new sense of the world, and this is the first step to being who we are truly meant to be. This will help us achieve the happiness and success we want, and we will be able to have the relationships that we always wanted. The saying is that when we don't look for it, we will find it.

The same can be said about success.

EPILOGUE

By simply thinking to ourselves about those early experiences we faced as children and how they affected us, we can use logic to break from the societal standards that have kept us locked up for so long. It is important to think about how we view ourselves. Do we believe we need to act a certain way to be valued by people? And if so, why do we put so much value on other people's opinions of us? Why are we afraid to think and act differently in front of others? Why do we care what others think?

If we could go back in time and tell our younger selves one thing, would it be to just be ourselves? That all the stuff we thought was important growing up wasn't? Would we tell ourselves that we deserve to be in a relationship with someone who loves us properly and without conditions? Would we say to have compassion for those who have lost their way because it easily could have been us if the circumstances were different? Would we say to have the courage to do what we want to do in life because that is what living life means? We are not living for other people. We are not carbon copies of the people who came before us. We do not have our fate set in stone by our parents and other members of society. We are our own people with our own interests, passions, and gifts. We are meant to explore our true potential in this life. We are meant to be happy by being ourselves.